Learning to Live

Loved

Learning to Live

*When a Fatherless Girl
Becomes a Christian Woman*

Delmesha L. Richards

Salted Ink
PUBLISHING
Pittsburgh

Learning to Live Loved
Published in the United States by Salted Ink Publishing
www.saltedinkpublishing.com

Hardcover ISBN 978-1-7339604-0-3
Paperback ISBN 978-1-7339604-1-0
E-book ISBN 978-1-7339604-2-7

Library of Congress Control Number: 2019904324

Dedication

To my dad, Daniel Thornton, the spiritual civil engineer God hired to play the essential role of an earthly father within the life of a broken, battered, and wounded young woman. You breathed life into my soul in ways only a father can, and never once did I fathom ever having the privilege of calling someone *Dad*. My life is significantly richer because you accepted God's call to father the fatherless, and I'll never be able to thank you enough for being the dad I never had. But, more importantly, you facilitated the most important relationship mankind could ever have; because of you, I have the ability to learn how to live loved by the ultimate Father of us all.

~

To my husband Ivan, the unmoving, unwavering, constant, consistent, and burden-bearing husband, who has loved me in ways that could only be fueled by the Holy Spirit residing in you. Your encouragement and firm belief in me has served as the wind beneath my wings. You get on my nerves every now and then, as only husbands can, but I am the woman I've become because of the man you've always been. The Lord knew who was capable of being an extension of His love for me within the covenant of marriage, and I will always choose you. I love you more than words can describe, and I apologize for comparing your "husbanding" to my dad during our first year of marriage! You truly come second to none. I love you. Cas

~

To my boys—Ivan Jr., Joseph, and Josiah—I love you all deeply and am becoming a better woman day by day because of the privilege and blessing of being your mom. I grow and progress in my relationship with the Lord because of you guys and will keep striving to be and give the very best of me. I love each of you with a love that only a mom can have.

To all the women growing and progressing in their Father-daughter relationship with the Lord. Every woman (and man) who grows up fatherless deserves to live within the perfect and matchless love of our Heavenly Father, and may each of us find that beautiful, sweet spot in Him and lean in for the rest of our natural lives.

~

"And for everyone with a red line under their name in Microsoft Word."
– Unknown

Table of Contents

Prologue

J don't remember exactly what day it was. I just know it was an afternoon in the spring of 2002. I was home on Spring Break in Pittsburgh visiting my family during my fourth year of college at South Carolina State University. My mom and I were on the east side of Pittsburgh driving through a neighborhood called Wilkinsburg. I wasn't really familiar with that side of town because I grew up on the Northside, but my mom knew it like the back of her hand because it was where she was raised—her old stomping grounds, as they say. While I was driving down one of the major avenues, taking in the urban and rugged sights, my mother looked straight ahead, pointed out her passenger side window, and said, "Your dad lives right there."

She was so flippant. The moment felt both odd and random because she and I never really discussed my father. The indifference in her voice and the calm carelessness in her body language felt rather eerie to me. Not only was I shocked and thrown completely off guard, all kinds of thoughts and emotions started making their way to the surface, but I had no time to really sit and sift through the waters that were beginning to flood my mind—let alone spend any time processing the gravity of what she had just revealed to me. The moment was swiftly escaping my grasp because the house she pointed to was moving farther away in my rearview mirror. So, I acted with an urgency that caused me to swerve and skid toward the sidewalk, a few blocks down from the house.

When the car came to a stop, I was in a slight state of panic, and my mom wasted no time as she began bickering and complaining. She became exasperated after I put the car in reverse, but I had no problem ignoring her because my mind was moving way too rapidly. I just wasn't capable of focusing on anything she was saying. I stopped my sky-blue Corolla at the curb directly in front of the house and could feel my armpits perspiring through my sweater—from my nervousness and growing indignation toward my father. I had no idea what I was going to do beyond knock on the door to see if he were there, and I certainly hadn't taken the time to consider what I might say to him. I was operating on sheer impulse and adrenaline.

Looking past my mom at his front door, disregarding what had become her own indignation, I placed the car in park. At that moment, she settled; I think she finally realized that all her outrage and pleading fell on deaf ears. I felt resolute, despite how ill-equipped I was, and my mom must have noticed the unwavering determination written all over my face.

I unbuckled my seatbelt, grabbed for the door handle, told my mom, "I'll be right back," as she scoffed and rolled her eyes at me. I approached the steps to the house and still had no idea what I wanted to say. Nor did I have a clue as to what I intended to gain from the soon-to-be awkward encounter with the man who conveniently walked out of my life over twenty years prior. Because of my impulse, I didn't take the time to consider whether he had a family or could have been contending with failing health or a dying parent. In that moment, none of that mattered to me as I became bent on looking him straight in the face with unhidden disgust and with the visible rage I could feel emerging to the surface of my stoic disposition.

Looking back, I guess the only objective I could muster on the fly, within those frenzied moments, was to prove (with my unannounced presence) that I was alive and doing well—that despite his absence and neglect, I managed to navigate through unpleasant circumstances within the city life that was intended to eat me alive and make me a statistic. Despite him, I got out with very few scratches and scrapes.

He needed to see the woman I was on the cusp of becoming, and I wanted him to grab a few glimpses of the tremendous successes awaiting me and, simultaneously, *grieve* the loss of the pride and joy only a loving parent could rightfully experience and lay claim to. He deserved to suffer somehow, and while I stood at his front door, my heart stood at attention, anticipating the moment the door would swing open.

That day, no one answered.

Chapter 1

Face to Face

The next day, I was determined to take full advantage of knowing where my father lived. I fully expected to see him face-to-face—and anyone else who dared to be around. My resolve to be a source of shame and embarrassment for him grew overnight, and it was exponential. I would be the mirror that reflected him as the irresponsible, deadbeat, loveless poor-excuse-for-a-father I believed he had to have been in order to abandon his own flesh and blood. And I didn't care what the circumstances could have been surrounding my abandonment. The little girl he turned his back on years ago would be the woman holding up the mirror that reflected the human monster he *was*. I couldn't wait!

In the afternoon, I selected my outfit and accessories with a little more care than usual. I pulled out my best pair of dark fitted, boot-cut jeans; a chunky ivory knitted sweater with intertwined shades of pinks, reds, blues, and golds; and my favorite rose pink ankle boots. I spent all my life hardly giving much thought to this man. One evening of mulling over the reality of his absence throughout my life caused a sudden and incredibly cold and dark corner of my heart to appear. I had asked myself all the typical questions—the hows and the whys—in an attempt to understand why he chose for me to live a life fatherless. Finding no reasonable answers within myself caused that cold, dark corner of my heart to balloon into something much more destructive.

As I daydreamed about our encounter, I became smitten with the scenario of my very presence sinking a knife into his heart, killing him softly. Using my gifted imagination, I visualized my out-of-state college education pulling the knife out and thrusting it back into his chest. I intended for my emotional distance and disgust to give the final devastating blow that would silence him and all the potential excuses he would attempt to conjure up when asked what I believed to be some very tough questions. To say the least, I was in a very dark place at this point.

For the first time in my life, I was experiencing a continual downpour of different types of emotions that had never knocked on the door of my heart before—at least not that I was aware of. The silent and unseen emotions that are attached to being unaccepted, rejected, abandoned, and unclaimed must have always been stirring throughout my life; I simply didn't realize this was what was taking place in my heart when I watched my childhood best friend cross the street to her house to greet her dad when he came home from work each afternoon. Seeing his car pull up in front of their home prompted her to move, and I always sat there and watched her walk over to him. I wondered what it felt like to call someone *Dad*. I wondered what it was like for her dad to interrupt her from playing Barbie dolls so she could hop in the family car, just the two of them, and drive off. Those things I never experienced, and over time I believed it caused my self-worth and self-esteem to diminish, despite the fact I, too, had these privileges—but only with my mom. What was it about me that didn't deserve to have my father be my dad?

My father walked out of my life around the time of my first birthday, according to my mom. Determining when, exactly, he stopped coming around and why he chose to make that decision depends on who's telling the story, but my greatest issue lies in the fact that, at some point, my father chose to no longer be a part of my life. Despite the circumstances, he made the choice to abandon me. He chose not to be active in my life, and I would become the only one of his seven children who grew up without his presence, without his love, without his guidance, and without his financial support. After I learned of his whereabouts—and the fact that he never moved residence my entire life—remembering this reality caused a sudden agony and affliction. This flood of emotions entered my heart the way a SWAT team enters an unsuspecting home, effectively disrupting everything through the element of surprise.

As late afternoon approached, I decided to get back in my car and make my way to the east side. I pulled up in front of the house again, but minus the anxiety and sweaty armpits. I stepped out of my Corolla, chirped the car alarm behind me, smoothed out my leather jacket, and took a deep breath while walking up to his door. I knocked a few times on his raggedy storm door and stood quietly, listening for any commotion taking place on the other side. I felt the corner of my lip curl up as I heard voices inside.

A young girl in her early teens opened the door. She had a familiar look: smooth yellow complexion with cute little freckles, sandy brown hair, a petite frame, and unassuming eyes. The innocence she carried and the familiarity of her face immediately disarmed me, and I greeted her with a genuine smile and a gentle voice, asking, "Hey! Is a Mr. Gerry here?"

"No," she said, "but my mom is here," and she stepped back, pulling on the main door, inviting me into her home. Without missing a beat, I opened the ragged storm door and stepped into what looked like a family room while she darted up a flight of steps calling for her mom. I reached behind me, closing both doors, but remained in the foyer. I felt a sense of disappointment at the fact that, again, my father wasn't home. But I decided it was a good thing that I was able to at least show myself to the adult who was present, regardless of who they were, and they would have no choice but to pass along the message of my appearance.

Not too much time passed before an attractive, fair-skinned woman with an urban roughness and a raspy voice came down the steps and walked toward me. As the woman moved closer, her facial expression indicated she recognized me! I observed her closely as her face passed through shock and disbelief and landed on pure delight. She opened her arms, and her joy was infectious. I smiled politely, while growing puzzled and unsure about what was taking place, and before I knew it, I was participating in a genuine embrace between what felt like two relatives.

I can't recall everything she said during the moments of her embrace, but I remember her repeating how she couldn't believe I was standing in her living room. The genuine warmth and unexpected beauty of the moment caused the intention of my heart toward my father to pause. Without taking a breath, she told me my father wasn't home but that he would be walking in the door shortly. The moment she spoke of him and his pending return, my heart slowly shifted back to the cold darkness that it was originally consumed by. I was reacquainted with my sole reason for being there in the first place.

While my heart was hardening back up, the woman invited me upstairs to their dining room to sit and talk until my father arrived. I followed behind her, and as I reached the top of the stairs, she introduced me to a group of people who were hanging out. She introduced herself as Ms. Dina and then introduced me to her daughter Lindsey, who was the young girl who answered the door. She then introduced me to her twin sons and a cousin they had adopted.

Greeting everyone politely on the outside, my heart thumped irregularly as I grappled with the fact that I had spent my entire life without this man. He missed every birthday and holiday, wasn't aware of my love for sports and dancing, missed every season, every game, and even my most prized championship games. He missed every track meet, every halftime show I danced in, and every sports banquet. He never challenged any of the boys who expressed an interest in me and had no hand in helping me navigate the complexities of the opposite sex. He never financially contributed to my livelihood and physical well-being. I never had the privilege of asking for a dollar so I could go to the corner store and pick out a dollar's worth of penny candy. But, he had the heart and ability to adopt another person's child!? Now that blew my mind!

We sat at the dining room table and made small talk, asking and answering surface questions, but I have to admit I enjoyed the attention! About fifteen to twenty minutes passed before the door downstairs opened and closed. Ms. Dina hollered from the table, "Gerry! Come upstairs. You'll never guess who's here."

I listened to his heavy and slow climb up the steps while gazing in anticipation at the corner where he would appear. My moment had finally arrived. My surroundings—and the congregated people around me—faded into a blurred background as my leg bounced, causing my body to sway from side to side. Slowly, a rather large, dark-skinned, gray-haired man appeared and turned the corner toward us, and shifted slowly across the floor. Looking around the room, he didn't notice me among his family, and I sat motionless in my seat, gazing at him—until his eyes met mine. The expression on his face shifted from the normalcy of just another end to his workday to a look that showed his entire world was slowing down. His eyes stayed fixed on me, and his slow, shuffling feet froze.

His face became still and silent, while his gaze was met with a stare influenced by a heart carrying hopes of burning a hole in his. He was not entertaining the innocent, resilient love of a longing daughter, who was simply resting at his dining room table among his wife and other children. He was unaware he stood gazing at a young woman enveloped in lovesick rage, the kind that only an abandoned child could carry. I sat there as a little girl, with hot-combed, straightened pigtails with yellow balls and barrettes. I sat there, the child who never knew his presence—the gifts of unconditional love, affirmation, protection, security, provision, and guidance that the other young teens sitting around me received. My quiet rage was bubbling in my soul because the man I would probably never call *Dad* stood in front of me, speechless.

Once he came to terms with who sat before him, he walked toward the table, and with no communication between the two of them, Ms. Dina stood up and walked around the table as he took her seat beside me. I have no idea whether everyone remained in the room, but I wouldn't be surprised if a silent suggestion from Ms. Dina caused everyone to remove themselves in an effort to leave us alone.

My father and I sat there having a very awkward conversation (at least for me). As he oozed over me with excitement, I sat there trying to balance my destructive emotions with how I was being embraced and loved on by everyone. I eventually became numb; I was overloaded from the warring and conflicting emotions within; they rendered me incapable of simply living in—and enjoying—the moment. He spent time sharing with me how much he loved me, and always had; he talked about how he always bragged about me to make sure everyone knew about me, because he carried me with him every day of his life. He gushed about how his wife and children knew so much about me—and loved me—because he made it a point to speak of me on a regular basis. He wanted to ensure I was always present in the minds and hearts of everyone he loved and held dear.

Obviously, I wasn't expecting any of this. This was not how I expected my encounter to unfold, and the detour mangled what I intended to take place. So, deciding not to let it deter me from gaining at least something, I took the opportunity to ask my father some very difficult questions. Unfortunately, I didn't have much of a listening ear or an open enough mind when it came to any of his responses; they fell on deaf ears. But one thing I noticed and remember vividly is that he never once said anything negative about my mother. He never once discredited her or tarnished her name, her actions, or her reputation. In fact, he did the very opposite. He went as far as declaring he still loved my mother and always would.

In the moment, I didn't value or appreciate him being that way toward my mother, but I do now. He took such care with his words when he spoke about her and their relationship, and he seemed to enjoy reminiscing about their time together. In that moment, I took inventory of my mother and her words regarding my father, and I couldn't remember her saying anything negative about him either. She usually bypassed talking about him and always mentioned the fact she was the one who ended the relationship. She also had very strong feelings and unpleasant words regarding his current wife. She often compared herself to Ms. Dina and always painted herself to be much more virtuous and honorable. I could never understand why my mother felt the need to always have something negative to say about Ms. Dina. I didn't know their history and I don't think there was much of one, outside of Ms. Dina being the woman my father eventually chose.

Nevertheless, my father was overjoyed at my being in his home, sitting and talking with him at his dining room table. He spent a lot of time trying to catch me up on a little more than twenty years of life. Most of it went in one ear and out the other because it was just way too much to take in. Although I didn't want to admit it to myself then, being told he loved me and that he had always loved me did something rather profound in my heart. My attitude didn't change as much as it could have, but it changed enough. The posture of my heart also shifted, but very slowly.

When I was ready to leave, we exchanged contact information and swapped sentiments of making it a point to stay in touch. I did manage to take the opportunity to express how everything was a bit much to adapt to and that it would take some time. He seemed very understanding. I had an immediate affection and affinity toward my siblings. Their adoration of me was palpable, and it really touched my heart. Plus, there were no reasons to have any hard feelings toward them. I guess I felt lucky to have them—and honored that they knew of me and referred to me as their big sister. That meant a lot and always will.

I was escorted downstairs and walked to my car, while the rest all assembled at the door and on the front porch. We waved and said more goodbyes as I entered my car and drove off. I found it interesting that if my father did, in fact, sense my indignation toward him, he didn't let on to it. He leaped right on over everything I was silently spewing in his direction, and he rode high above where I existed, thoroughly enjoying himself. During our conversation, he took the opportunity to tell me he knew that someday I would arrive on his doorstep. On one hand, I took comfort in him saying that because I've always believed that there are three sides to a story—his, hers, and the truth—but I also felt sadness because it didn't agree with me that I had to be the one arriving at his doorstep. It could and should have been him arriving at mine. How can adults, especially absent parents, expect the child(ren) to take on the responsibility of reaching out and reconnecting? Especially after living the majority of life without ever having felt their presence.

I walked away from that encounter believing that, at some point, my father and I would have the opportunity to dig into the details regarding his choice to not play a significant part in my life. He was so open and willing to talk about the past, and I hoped that when that time finally came, he would understand that I truly didn't care about any of the events or reasons behind the demise of his relationship with my mother. All that mattered to me was the fact that he chose to raise his three daughters before me, his daughter and two sons after me, and even an adopted relative, while forsaking me! He needed to answer to this. And he would come to know that I needed him to fully acknowledge that he abandoned me—and in my mind, it would only be right if, at some point, he asked for my forgiveness. Which I would be more than willing to give.

Chapter 2

Three Sides to Every Story

I would love to believe that meeting my biological father (Gerry) for the first time as an adult and being around his accepting family meant more to me than it actually did. My time with them certainly left a beautiful impression on me; there was a glimmer of hope in my heart, but our encounter didn't make much of an impact on me and my overall outlook on life. At the time I met Gerry, I was in a really dark place in my life and had a long road ahead of me, and the years following our encounter proved we had nothing more than a surface-level relationship. He skipped out on me, missing my entire life up to that point, and I was still fatherless. I may have been a twenty-one-year-old young woman residing out of state, attending college, but I still needed a dad. I still needed him to step up to the plate, put forth some effort to get to know me, assess where I was in life, and begin fathering me right from where I stood. The road may not have been a cakewalk, but it could have been! More than anything, I believe I was worth it for him to at least make a real effort, but the most I received through the years was his side of the story.

I had the privilege of talking to both my mom and Gerry about different aspects of their relationship, and they were both pretty open and transparent. I sat with my mom at Longhorn Steakhouse one afternoon and asked her a series of questions I had prepared in advance. I took notes on my laptop as we sat and talked. It was such a joy having the opportunity to "interview" my mom. Her answering all my questions in such detail was mind-blowing; she hid nothing and had no shame, laying everything bare right there on the table between us. I had quite a few "wow, really?" and "wow, reeaaaally!" moments—and I had several raised-eyebrow moments that turned to deeply furrowed eyebrows as she walked me down memory lane. I even heard some sheer foolishness at times!

It was great having the ability to ask Gerry all the same questions, but not all at one time. When I left Pittsburgh after spring break and returned to South Carolina to finish my last semester, I talked every now and then with him. I relocated to Washington DC, and whenever I visited home, I made it a point to stop by his house. He often repeated himself during our discussions; he seemed to really love reminiscing with me. It wasn't a bother initially, but after a while it got on my nerves because that's what dominated all our conversations. Again, he wasn't taking any time to get to know me and what was going on in my life, how I was progressing. And he offered me nothing in the way of fatherly advice or counsel. But even still, it's hard to describe just how much I appreciated having both sides of the story—and the fact that I got them so freely and willingly. So I value both perspectives equally, because they put me in the unique position of traveling right down the middle, piecing together my own opinion.

She Said . . .

Within my family, it's no secret that I'm the product of an adulterous affair. I am a love child. My mom was about nineteen years old with a toddler son, and Gerry was an older married man, with three daughters, working as a carpenter instructor at a trade school called Bidwell Training Center. My mother was only about four years older than his oldest daughter! According to my mom, she herself was attending the trade school for their electrical engineering program when a friend of hers named Pete mentioned that Gerry had taken an interest in her. She thought, *He's a teacher, he's driving a Lincoln, and I could use some extra money.* This was probably the first of my many raised-eyebrow moments. My mom was living with a close friend and shared with her that she saw Gerry as a sugar daddy. She began stopping by his classroom; they went out to eat, drank together, enjoyed the party scene and other events around the city. He let her know he was married with three daughters, and when I asked how she felt about him being married, she shrugged and said, "I didn't feel anything." She felt he was out doing his thing and she was okay with that.

My mother didn't have a stable living arrangement for her and my older brother; she bounced between friends' apartments and her dad. At one point, Gerry got a place she could afford. She and Gerry moved in together, but she eventually moved back with her dad, and Gerry went home to his wife. Her father was aware of their relationship but wasn't aware Gerry was married. While she was saving up money for an apartment of her own, she loaned Gerry money to pay a bill; her dad found out about the loan and was extremely upset because at this point, he came into the knowledge that Gerry was a married man. When Gerry came to visit, her dad ran him out of the house with a rifle, enraged that his daughter was helping to support a married man and his family. But she didn't care much about what her father felt because by then she was in love with Gerry.

During her stay with her dad, she was accused of stealing money (which her stepbrother actually stole), and she was kicked out. She and my brother bounced around a few more times until her dad got in touch with her to let her know a Section 8 apartment was available for her in a housing project called Fineview. My mom and her dad reconciled after he apologized, admitting he was wrong about her stealing money. He also acknowledged that kicking her out was wrong. He brought her gifts and took her out every now and then, which allowed things to go back to normal.

The dynamic between my mom and Gerry is bizarre to me as she talked about the dynamic between her and Gerry's wife and daughters.

She recalled going to see the Temptations in concert with Gerry and his eldest daughter. She watched their younger two daughters and braided their hair, washed their clothes, sent food, and sometimes sent food stamps to his wife whenever she called. This is the foolishness I was talking about that had my eyebrows deeply furrowed. But that's how it was, and she has no regrets, nor shame.

Finally moving into her own apartment, my mom recalled only having a few of the basics, like pots and pans, dishes, pallets to sleep on, etc. Gerry helped her furnish her apartment and eventually moved in. She got pregnant, but she didn't want the baby because Gerry was still married, and—despite him expressing the desire for her to keep it—she got an abortion. A year went by, and she ended up pregnant with me, deciding that she couldn't go forward with another abortion. Late in her pregnancy, Gerry went to hook up a washer and dryer for his wife, which took him two months to finish. He finally returned, and at that point, my mom decided he would need to show her he was serious about her and their relationship. She gave him an ultimatum; he didn't have to marry her, but he had to divorce his wife by the time I turned one. He agreed and moved back in. A month before my birthday, she caught him cheating with yet another woman and still didn't end their relationship because he had one more month to make good on his word to divorce his wife. During this part of the conversation, I wondered if my mom was somewhat of a doormat, and when I asked her, she shrugged with sheer nonchalance on her face and replied, "I was just young and dumb I guess."

One week before my first birthday, he still wasn't divorced. My mother ended their relationship and told him he needed to leave her apartment.

Gerry left and returned sporadically to retrieve his things. At one point, it got physical between them, and my mom called two of her siblings to intervene. She moved on by dating someone they both knew, a guy named Robert. This was an effort to get back at Gerry since she knew he didn't want their relationship to be over. When her relationship with Robert ended, Gerry came 'round to give her money and often picked me and my brother up to take us places. However, when she moved on to another relationship, she felt Gerry was becoming unreasonable—showing up unannounced, questioning her, wanting to know who was around or what was new in her house, etc. At some point, Gerry got into an altercation with her then latest boyfriend that turned bloody (for the boyfriend) and involved the police. My mom said she eventually got rid of them both, telling Gerry she didn't want or need his money and to stop coming around completely. Which he did.

Years later, my mom decided to take Gerry to court for child support. She said the first time she sued him, I was in middle school, and because he was on disability, she wasn't awarded much. Some time passed, and she was told by one of Gerry's relatives that he came into some money and he had also opened a convenience store on his side of town. She sued for child support a second time when I was in high school, and they sent her eighteen dollars a month. She didn't think he was being honest with the courts but decided she wouldn't fight it.

He Said . . .

Gerry tells an almost identical story, but his details between the main events are very different. When I asked him to describe how they met, he shared that—while teaching at the trade school—everywhere he went he saw my mom's head peeping around the corner and she often hung out by his classroom door. One day, a counselor came to him to say my mother liked something about him, and to advise Gerry to let her transfer to his room because she'd pay attention to everything he said. This was my first raised-eyebrow moment during this conversation! Gerry agreed to the transfer.

My mother often brought my brother to school with her, and Gerry would give them a ride to a part of town called The Hill, where she was staying—a hotel where bad girls hung out. He didn't want her staying there, and he talked about a friend who had a place with rooms available, so he rented her one. His friend ended up having "ill intentions" toward my mom, but she assured Gerry nothing happened between them. He believed her but wanted her to have her own place and helped her get her first apartment in the Fineview housing project.

When my mother moved into her apartment, she asked Gerry to stay with her, but he let her know he'd only be able to stay sometimes because he had obligations at home. He went on to talk about his marriage, how he and his wife weren't in love anymore and didn't get along. They tried marriage counseling, where he discovered she would only split herself between their kids, herself, and her career as a novelist, leaving nothing for him and their relationship. He tried sticking around but developed an ulcer, and was advised by his doctor to find ways to get out, have fun, and enjoy life. Otherwise, he would have a premature death.

Meeting my mom gave him that fun, joy, and excitement. When I asked Gerry if my mother gave him money for his family, he admitted there were times he didn't have money for his daughters and she did give them things, but she did so much more for him. He described the different places they went together, from parties and bars to movies and roller-skating. She managed to get him on her softball team, even though he couldn't catch a ball to save his life. He said whenever they entered a room, the entire atmosphere shifted, and he loved every moment.

Gerry talked about wanting to meet my mother's father, and despite being warned that my grandfather was really mean, he persisted. When he got the opportunity to meet my grandfather, Gerry asked him about not caring for his grandson (my brother) and served as a mediator who facilitated my grandfather allowing my mother to move back in with him. But one day she tried cooking and almost burned the house down, which resulted in her getting kicked out. Gerry tried to smooth things over for her, but my grandfather was enraged and left the room. My mother knew he left the room to retrieve his shotgun, so she warned Gerry and they escaped.

When my mother got pregnant with me, they continued going to different places and enjoying the social scene together until she was too big, which was around her seventh or eighth month. He never left, and when she went into labor, he was in the hospital with her and continued living with my mother until I was one. On my first birthday, he went to buy a birthday cake but came back to meet his clothes on the front porch in garbage bags. She told him to leave and go back to his wife, but he pushed his way into the apartment and saw his best friend, Robert, in the apartment. Although he wanted to hurt Robert, he was advised against it by his niece and decided to grab his bags and head home, where he lived by himself. I asked Gerry about the ultimatum my mom said she gave him about divorcing his wife by the time I turned one, and he said he doesn't remember my mother giving him an ultimatum.

But he did speak on how he wasn't sure about divorcing his wife, and for a couple of reasons. On one hand, he knew my mom didn't want to be married and knew she was a "parkway," meaning that it was only a matter of time before she would be ready to take an exit. While on the other hand, he knew that because he was disabled, divorcing his wife would cause him to lose everything—and all for a younger woman who was wild and wouldn't likely be in the picture much longer.

Once the relationship was over, Gerry moved on. He never called my mother about visiting; he just showed up with gifts for me and brought money to my mother every month. He and his girlfriend even brought dresses for me one Christmas. But one day he found himself in a physical altercation with one of my mother's boyfriends. At that point, he decided it was necessary to deal with the situation a different way, so he stopped coming around and had a mutual friend give my mother the things I needed and wanted.

Years later, he received a letter regarding a lawsuit for back child support and went to court. He had a briefcase that kept records of everything he did and receipts for everything he gave. He later received papers from the judge, advising him to file for custody of me, but he told the judge no because my mother was a good mother and he had no desire to do something like that to her. So, the judge ordered child support for twelve dollars a month. My mother tried suing him again for financial support, but that time I was eighteen, and the judge threw the case out at Gerry's request.

What I say . . .

In a nutshell, they were both right and they were both wrong, as far as I'm concerned. The absolute truth will always evade me, which is actually okay since their recollection of the events are so similar. They both could have handled themselves differently, and they certainly should have handled me differently. It's really unfortunate to see how this is yet another situation where both parents are more concerned with preserving their own interests and placing their personal preferences above the overall well-being of the child. They both failed miserably.

My mom was clearly immature and incapable (perhaps unwilling, even) of seeing, understanding, or valuing a child's need for the presence and active role of a father (my brother's father wasn't in his life either). She was a fiercely independent and free-spirited young woman who came up on the streets, not answering to anyone but herself. I have no doubt in my mind that although she was deeply in love with Gerry, when she decided the relationship was over, she was the stick-a-fork-in-me kind of done. She was not about to relinquish any of her control when it came to her child(ren), and she couldn't care less about his opinion or input concerning me. She had no interest in allowing Gerry to father me in his own way, and co-parenting with him was not something she cared about in the least bit. In fact, I doubt either of them had any concept of what a healthy co-parenting relationship even looked like.

Staying out of her way and her business while bringing her money and taking me (and my brother) out was probably her standard for their situation, while his intentions were probably a lot more intrusive than was probably reasonable.

But I do give them both the benefit of the doubt in some areas. For my mom, she may have been willing to grow into a pleasant co-parenting relationship with Gerry if he were a different kind of man. He was older and more experienced than she. He had a different moral compass, and he didn't hesitate to speak his mind. He was probably more fatherly than she cared for, considering they were no longer in a relationship, so she probably began to despise any opinion or perspective he attempted to offer. He probably tried to use me as a way to control some of the things about her that he may not have held in high regard, but her priority would always be to have the freedom to do whatever she wanted to do, as she always did. And if that meant I would live life without my father, so be it. She was not the caliber of woman to facilitate a relationship between me and Gerry apart from her personal feelings toward him or her preferences concerning her household and privacy. Unfortunately, my balance and well-being weren't her ultimate priority (at least not in this situation).

My mom strongly believed she was more than capable of raising her two children alone, and despite how hard it would get, she had the strength within herself to dig her heels into the ground, push against any obstacle in her way, and rise above any circumstance that attempted to drown her or her children. Unfortunately, she would never truly understand the role she played in facilitating her children in accumulating years of damage that we would spend much of our adult years trying to unravel, release, and heal from. The best mother in the world can never replace or fulfill anything a father is designed and purposed to provide—physically, emotionally, mentally, or spiritually. This is just a matter of fact. Although I understand where she was coming from, considering who I know her to be, I vehemently disagree with how she handled—and in many ways, blocked—Gerry being in my life.

But in the same breath, I do place a majority of the responsibility of my fatherlessness on him. After all, it was his ultimate decision to walk away and leave his child. Not only was he older and wiser, he had years of parenting under his belt in comparison to my mother. As far as I can tell, he is a very mildmannered, soft-spoken man, and I appreciate his stance on not wanting to bring—or be the source of—drama in my life. But when all the dust settled, the fact remains: he took an easier route that resulted in me living a life without a father. I do feel as though he had a few interesting gaps in his side of the story; a few things don't quite add up within his time line, but I have no doubt in my mind that my mother didn't make it easy for him to see or have me. I wouldn't put it past her to have even kept me from him out of her own bitterness and spite. I have no doubt in my mind that he loved me and expected to be a part of my life for the duration but genuinely didn't want to be near the drama and violence that surrounded him and his association with my mother.

Over time, I think Gerry settled with his new girlfriend, finally got his divorce, remarried, and began having more kids. His primary focus likely shifted to his new family, just as it shifted away from his first wife and family when he and my mother got involved. As he neglected his first family, his second family would feel that same type of neglect. My mom eventually started dating a mild-mannered family man with a good job, who eventually moved her out of the projects. His name was Mr. Billy, and he was a stable, solid guy. But my father never came back around. I don't mean to be unfair toward Gerry, but I'm adamant in feeling he should have fought to be in my life, come hell or high water. Even if he felt the need to take a break for a couple of years to let the dust settle on both sides before making his way back to me. I believe my mom eventually grew up, matured, and become stable within herself, at least enough for him to manage being consistent and present in my life.

Or perhaps he did attempt to come back in his own way. When I was in middle school, he called my mom's house, and I'm assuming this was prompted by the child support lawsuit my mom filed against him. Granted, it's unfortunate that a child support lawsuit could be the catalyst for him trying to come around, but it is what it is. I remember my mom called me downstairs and had the phone in her hand, telling me it was my dad, and she asked if I wanted to talk to him. I remember her tone was laced with disgust and her body language reflected that same negative vibe, and I'm certain that if they were different, I would have likely agreed to talk with him. I had no reason not to. Her energy influenced me; I took my cue from her and declined to talk with him. She pulled the phone back up to her ear, and I watched her, with a proud smugness, tell Gerry I didn't want to talk to him and then hung up the phone. In hindsight, I can't even begin to imagine the disappointment, and the potential heartache, he may have felt. But he continued with the idea that it was reasonable for him to sit and wait until I showed up on his doorstep.

Looking back, when my mom called me downstairs to see if I wanted to talk with Gerry on the phone, I wish I had told her yes. What if we could have started developing a relationship then? There is a chance we could have developed something meaningful, and I would have had the opportunity to grow up alongside my younger siblings. Instead, when I finally reached his doorstep and crossed his threshold, I had already reached my breaking point in life. I was bobsledding down an icy slope, and if I had not been diverted by a relative at the time, there's no telling who I would be or where my life would be today.

When I finally showed up at twenty-one years old, my life was in peril. Every meaningful friendship I had by then had either ended or was on the verge of ending. I had destroyed my academic career and reputation—and burned all my bridges with the professors who saw me as a rising star and had taken an interest in cultivating my future career within the business and IT industry. I was no longer interested in monogamy. After the pain of rejection from my college sweetheart, I decided the single life was for me, along with the social and sexual freedom that came with it. I lost my job as a bartender after they accused me of creatively stealing money from them . . . which I had been.

With everything falling apart, the most pressing of them all was being strapped for money. I connected with the sister of a friend who happened to be a stripper. Getting a job as a waitress at the Cracker Barrel paled in comparison to the fast money she talked about. Since I was living free and had lost most of my inhibitions, going that route was a shoulder shrug as I moved forward with my decision to make a living by taking my clothes off around a pole. My plans to hit the stage were interrupted, thanks to spring break and the intervention of my sister-in-law, who helped me with my financial situation—so long as I gave her my word that I wouldn't become a stripper. I gave my word, took the cash, made my way back to South Carolina, and about thirty days later, I gave my life to the Lord.

I connected with Gerry right in the midst of this! He was aware of where my life was and my plans to become a stripper. He shared how much he didn't want that for me, but that was about all he offered. He wasn't much of a brake for my bobsled; he played no significant role in slowing my swift decline, and through the years, he has taken no part in my rise from the bottom. He hasn't offered me anything valuable and useful in the way of fatherly advice, insight, wisdom, or Godly counsel (being that he is a Christian)—and each of our conversations remained very surface and dominated by his reminiscing about the past.

Maybe I'm wrong for desiring him to be more than what he has been. Maybe I'm being unfair in my expectation and assessment of him, that what he has given over the years—since reconnecting—hasn't even been a drop in the bucket.

But then again, since this is the truth of my heart, maybe I'm not wrong or being unfair.

Chapter 3

A Fatherless Bedrock

*G*rowing up with a single mother was a life common among many of my peers. I noticed I was living without a dad within the normalcy of my day to day; however, I took special notice of my family and friends who had their fathers in their homes—or at least knew their fathers and had relationships with them. I'm pretty sure I've always had some inclination that growing up without a father affected me in some way, but I was never aware of the type of impact his absence had on me through the years. It was something I hardly spent time pondering, so I just assumed that whatever the impact, it must be pretty minimal.

I was still in my early twenties when I realized I may be grappling with more significant "daddy issues." The primary way I discovered this was through my longing to be married while going through a long series of failed relationships. I was a babe in Christ gleaning from the teachings of a youth pastor named Tejado Hanchell. He led the singles ministry at my church when I was living in Washington DC. He was holding one of his events for the singles of the church, which was primarily made up of college students from Howard University and young working professionals like myself. During the discussion, he took a tangent from his topic and mentioned how important and beneficial it is to speak to a professional about the issues that often plague us, especially as Christians. He talked a lot about how we often disregard—for various reasons—the idea of therapy and counseling, and he took the time to list many of the benefits he had both studied while pursuing a higher-level degree in Christian counseling and personally experienced. At one point, he said it's extremely helpful to just be able to sit down with a trained person and do nothing more than talk.

That certainly piqued my interest, especially since I had never sat with anyone and just talked about my life. After the event, I asked him if he had any recommendations, and he pointed me in the direction of a Christian counseling center in Silver Spring, MD, which was less than a thirty-minute metro ride from my apartment in DC. I didn't have any of the hang-ups Minister Hanchell highlighted as common among the Christian community, especially the black Christian community, nonetheless, I became a client almost immediately. My first few sessions were helpful; being able to release my pent-up thoughts and emotions freed me mentally and emotionally, which was really encouraging. But it didn't last long because I began having some hang-ups with the counselor and her push for me to be diagnosed as bipolar and clinically depressed. I knew I was neither of these; I was well aware I simply needed assistance working through the mental, emotional, and psychological effects of being fatherless.

At some point, it was clear that her push for a diagnosis was to ensure she could continue to make claims against my medical insurance so she would continue receiving payment. It was something the industry required of her, despite it being a faith-based practice, but that didn't sit well with me and it still doesn't. Don't get me wrong, I'm all about being paid for your time and services. Get your money! But in that situation, I believe it put me in a position to be forced into a specific category of mental illness that wasn't accurate, and if my diagnosis was inaccurate, my subsequent treatment (both therapy and prescribed medicine) would be off. I did not want to waste time being treated for something that was not likely the root of my issue. I would have rather spent time seeing if counseling alone would help with any form of depression she felt I may have been experiencing. Especially before prescribing medicine. If within the time allotted, I showed I wasn't making any progress in my "condition," then send along the little green pills. But when she tried to combine the bipolar with depression and pills, I immediately felt something wasn't right, and I'm thankful I followed that instinct and gut feeling. I have to add, though, that mental illness is real. Many of us suffer from various types brought on for different reasons, and I am in no way opposed to being properly diagnosed and treated by a professional. In many instances, prescribed medicine is necessary, and I hope the stigma surrounding mental illness will continue to decline as it has been these past few years. However, I am vehemently opposed to frivolous, irresponsible, and profit-driven healthcare in all forms.

From Some to Most

Needless to say, I stopped going to counseling and decided to do some exploring and reading of my own. I had no idea of the massive amount of data, research, and statistics that existed on the topic of father absence and the effects it has on different groups of children on into adult life. A lot of the information was interesting to sift through, and I received some comfort in knowing there were issues that are common among most fatherless children. I appreciated the reminder that my fatherlessness was not unique, my situation wasn't an anomaly, and the ways I may be affected could likely be identified and addressed.

During the course of my reading and research, I determined within myself that I didn't quite fit into most of the categories researchers concluded were common among individuals who grew up with an absent father. Those primary categories are:

- Raised in Poverty
- Truancy and Poor Academic Performance
- Drug and Alcohol Abuse
- Homelessness & Mental Disorders
- Promiscuity and Teen Pregnancy
- Behavioral and Social Problems (inability to build healthy relationships)

- Crime and Entrance into the Justice System
- Abusive Relationships
- Low Self-Esteem and Self-Worth
- Lack of Physical and Emotional Security
- Exploitation and Abuse (molestation and rape)
- Physical Health Issues

As far as I was concerned, I didn't fall into hardly any of these categories, and the few that I did weren't a result of father absence. For instance, I never had poor academic performance but excelled throughout school and most of college. I never suffered from mental disorders or physical health issues, I was never molested as a child, and I always felt safe and secure under the arm and protection of my mother. I was never promiscuous or pregnant, never abused drugs or alcohol, was never in trouble with the law, and had never been homeless.

Make no mistake, I never felt or believed that life for me was full of colorful flowers and succulent grapes. But as I dug into the data, I genuinely couldn't relate. The research became unhelpful to me because it was no longer providing me with insight into my specific situation and potential impact. I had a similar impression after I picked up a book released by Jonetta Rose Barras titled *Whatever Happened to Daddy's Little Girl?: The Impact of Fatherlessness on Black Women*. I thoroughly enjoyed reading her story and the insight she provided from her personal experience as a fatherless woman; I was glued to her book during my metro commute to and from work. But, much like the research, I wasn't able to pull anything useful from her book that related to me personally.

It didn't leave me with anything more than an enjoyable time reading the fatherless experience from another woman's perspective once she came to the realization she was affected by the absence of her father.

Not until close to fifteen years later am I able to look back and see much clearer just how much I actually fell into quite a few of the categories outlined by those researchers of fatherless children. I believe there are always blind spots, especially when our specific and unique variables don't seem to be accounted for in the grand scheme of things. In some instances, the categories felt extreme, and the view I had of myself and my personal outlook on life just didn't seem to fit. Especially when, in other cases, I knew people who fell into many of those categories in a much more direct way. Not fitting into those categories as some of the other folks I knew allowed me to disassociate myself from certain categories altogether. Ultimately, I was just self-deceived, thinking more highly of myself (and my circumstances). Over the years, I suppressed or had completely forgotten many of the facts and situations that accurately depicted the truth about me. Besides, who wants to be labeled or placed into a category that's not a positive reflection of what they think or believe about themselves (and their past)? The variables that make my life and situation unique matter greatly, but not so much that I should disregard the overarching truth and/or dismiss my overall reality, no matter how uncomfortable or jarring it is. To discover and identify the root of every issue I have is paramount and can't be avoided. At least not forever.

Fast forward to a couple years later. I was finally found by my husband, Ivan, and together we walked into a Christ-centered marriage. After about two years, we relocated from Washington, DC, to Pittsburgh, and a new situation (discussed in a later chapter) prompted me to pursue counseling again. This time around, I began seeing a Christian counselor who didn't accept health insurance! During a few of our sessions, she and I were able to pinpoint and discuss how fatherlessness served as the bedrock for many of my dysfunctions. In many instances, the absence of my father planted seeds that later grew into a jungle of various pits, hurdles, and obstacles I had to learn to either maneuver through or live with the best way I knew how.

I also had to work through a workbook, which is where I discovered that growing up without a father more than likely opened the door for me to be sexually assaulted my freshman year in college. I wasn't necessarily starving for the love and attention of a boyfriend, because I had that; boyfriends were pretty easy to come by (but that's not to say those relationships were healthy). But, for me, fatherlessness actually served as the initial puncture in my soul that led to me being in the position of starving for the interest, attention, guidance, and selfless love of a man who would want nothing from me in return. These are the very circumstances and the emotional hunger within that eventually led to me being naïve about a person who would later violate me. I did fall into the category of exploitation and abuse after all. The puncture of my father's absence led to more than a decade-long bleed that would eventually grow into a hemorrhage that spilled onto and soiled every area of my life. It influenced and informed all my decisions and behaviors because it colored the lens through which I observed and experienced life, people, circumstances, and behaviors (both my own and others).

I believe that my story is no more unique than the millions of women within each generation also touched by fatherlessness. We all carry the backdrop of growing up without a father and are affected in very similar ways, while at the same time being drastically different in how we are marked and influenced by the same circumstances. The varied nature in how fatherlessness can shape us is often seen through the single mothers that raise us. The wisdom, strength, resilience, and resourcefulness—or lack thereof—of our single mothers will undoubtedly have a drastic effect on how severe father absence affects us. And the involvement—or lack thereof—of our extended family, village, or support system, cultivated by our mothers, has a significant influence as well.

Unfortunately, my mother didn't have much of a support system or village, and she grew up having endured various traumas after losing her mother to cancer at the age of nine. Although she had her dad in her life, that didn't afford her the stability she required and the guidance and resources she needed. Despite her past, my mother made it a point to ensure my older brother and I wouldn't lack in the many ways she did. Growing up, and well into my high school years, I was never aware of any lack of resources. My mother was a single, stay-at-home mom, and we always had a clean, furnished house, ate three meals a day plus snacks, dressed nicely, and never had a shortage of activities to enjoy during the seasons of summer (e.g., swimming, amusement parks, picnics) and winter (e.g., roller-skating, ice-skating, museums). Life was good, as far as I knew. Later, I learned that we grew up living in Section 8 housing, and my mother received food stamps and other government benefits. It wasn't until 1996, as a result of former President Bill Clinton signing into law the Personal Responsibility and Work Opportunity Reconciliation Act, that my mother was trained, and she entered into the workforce for the first time.

Despite my mother's best efforts, we grew up in poverty, according to national measurements of resources. I now realize that I belong to another category common among fatherless children. I take into consideration everything my mom sacrificed, but my mother could never give that which only a father could provide. So not only did Gerry's abandonment dig a number of empty, emotional pits in my life that would only increase over time, he also didn't support me financially. I became curious about his financial support while walking with my older brother through his custody battles for his eldest son. After asking my mom about whether Gerry financially supported me, she gave me an emphatic *no*—after a moment of laughter. I believed her, but I still wanted to check for myself, so I contacted the courts in Pittsburgh and requested the court documents, which were mailed to me. I was able to see with my own eyes how he was never forced (by the legal system) to provide any substantial child support. "On the books," Gerry lacked income, and he has been disabled for years, but I have also seen with my own eyes his knack for entrepreneurial activities in order to support himself and his family. However, growing up, I had no idea what it felt like to be provided for by anyone other than my mother.

During my last two years of high school, life felt like nighttime in the deep South, smothering and pitch black. My mother picked up on living her best life as the socialite she must have been suppressing while she was in the trenches of raising her two kids as a teen and young mother. Our relationship became extremely volatile because she just didn't seem like the woman I knew anymore. Once I reached the age of fifteen, she was no longer the sole provider of everything I needed and wanted. She was no longer the mother that never missed a game; I stopped hearing her yells from the sideline. She didn't provide any financial support for any of the dances or extracurricular activities I got involved in. So by the time my senior year rolled around, I wanted to get as far away from my mother as I possibly could. Literally!

A friend named Alexis Howard went on a Black College Tour through the high school, and she came back to school one day losing her mind, raving about this one particular school in South Carolina that had palm trees on campus and people that spoke in wonderful Southern accents. As she raved about this school, I decided that was where I would attend college. I did no research of my own, and I had no idea what city or town the school was located in or how long of a drive it was from Pittsburgh. I didn't know how much it cost per year to attend the school, I had no idea what the school's academic strengths and reputation were, and I didn't speak to anyone about my decision. I just made it happen, and in the fall of 1998, I made plans to travel to Orangeburg, South Carolina, to begin my college education at South Carolina State University (SCSU). My mother and uncle drove me to the school with as much of my belongings as I could fit in his truck. After spending the day with me, my mom left me with a card that had a handwritten note inside that read, "I knew we needed space, but it didn't have to be this far." At the time, my heart was too hardened to realize or appreciate what my mom was trying to express. It was just time for me to move on.

Nighttime Turned Midnight

College is where life's curveballs were no longer just throwing me for a loop; after a while they connected and every now and then forced me to drop into the dirt. During my second semester as a freshman, I found myself filled by the attention of an upperclassman who was soon to be graduating from the School of Business, which is where I was majoring. He was someone I genuinely believed took an interest in me, mirroring that of a big brother and mentor. He freely shared his knowledge of the School of Business, my instructors, the curriculum and classes, campus life, etc. He was pouring water into a few of those empty pits I accumulated over the years, and like a sundried sponge, I soaked up every drop, believing I was gaining what I never had before: a male who was selflessly interested in my overall well-being and future success, with no desire or expectation of benefit for himself. Him having any desires or motives other than seeing me succeed never once crossed my mind. But things with this upperclassman didn't end well for me. One evening, he sexually assaulted me.

From the moment he was done until years later, I never told a soul, suffering alone and in silence. Two semesters later, I was living temporarily in Greenville, South Carolina, taking advantage of an internship at a company called Bowater Inc. I shared a house with two other people, and one afternoon I decided to take my life. I was tired of bearing the burden I placed on myself for allowing myself to be assaulted; I grew tired of the internal struggle, strife, and suffering. I believed wholeheartedly that being raped was my fault because I lacked the common sense and wisdom that would have prevented it from happening. And I was carrying the shame of having a mother who had been tireless in ensuring I would never endure the trauma of molestation . . . only to be raped the moment I chose to leave from under her wing of protection. With the sexual assault and suicide attempt, I effectively fell into two more categories researchers listed for fatherless children.

Being sexually assaulted caused my view and perspective of the world and people around me to diminish severely. I saw my roommates and closest friends through angry eyes for failing to sense something was wrong with me the evening I returned to my dorm. My relationship with my high school sweetheart deteriorated and eventually ended, and my social life took a steep downward spiral as the person I had always been changed. I remember riding in the car with a male friend, and at some point within our conversation, he looked me square in my eyes and said, "You've changed." By then I was stone cold on the inside, and his observation and words didn't affect me one bit. And they should have.

My desire and ability to love, to be emotionally invested, and to receive love from other women evaporated, and romantic relationships with men became majorly dysfunctional. I decided, by any means necessary, I would always be in control and would never again be found helpless or in a situation where I couldn't control my environment. I became fearless when in the presence of males, whether they were my peers or slightly older than me. I was fueled by the internal rage of being taken advantage of as a result of my own stupidity. I decided I would never again be found unsuspecting, timid, or naïve. Never again would I experience the fear and dread that consumed me to the point of paralysis like I experienced the night of the assault. The last thing I would ever do was duplicate any part of my temperament that led to that situation. I swung like a pendulum toward the other end of the spectrum. My number of sexual partners began to rise slowly as I lived freely as a single college girl. I could now add myself to three more categories.

During the remainder of my years in college, my grades dropped, and making the dean's list evaporated; I lost interest in my studies, and my class attendance dropped. I never enjoyed the taste of alcohol, and boy, did I try! So, my alternative coping mechanism was diving head first into the daily use of marijuana. I became a part of "Team Wake 'N Bake" and effectively strolled into another two categories.

Blind Spots and Self-Deception

I have to admit, I still have trouble seeing how the various categories I do fit into are a result of father absence. Sometimes it's hard to recognize the fatherless link because I didn't slip into most of those categories until after I experienced the trauma of rape while in college. For the most part, I sailed through my childhood and high school years, but when I take the time to stop basking in the good memories and start reflecting and digging up memories, I would much rather remain in the abyss—yet, I can also see the other side of my reality.

I read an article called "Emotional Hunger vs. Love," and the author described emotional hunger as "a strong, emotional need caused by deprivation in childhood."[1] Most times, it's extremely difficult for me to see how specifically I was deprived by my father's absence because the task of reflecting, sifting, and piecing things together is such a huge undertaking. Even for someone like me. I pride myself on being this very type of person—a reflector, sifter, and "piecer-together!" I only began recognizing my deprivation and deficits once I journeyed through the jungle of trying to see, understand, and relate to God as my Heavenly Father. My idea of Him as a Father is painfully vague and superficial at best. How am I supposed to see and relate to God as *my father* when I have absolutely no reference point? I've never been able to offer anything meaningful to our Father-daughter relationship because the majority

---

1 Robert W. Firestone, "Emotional Hunger vs. Love," February 24, 2009, Psychology Today (website). www.psychologytoday.com.

of my life as a believer has been relating to Him as the omnipotent, omnipresent, and omniscient being that He is.

Through my religious experience, I learned how to relate to God as Lord, Savior, King, and Master—and in some instances, a dictator who still happens to be pretty friendly most times. I understood His capacity to love unfathomably and perfectly, but I had moments when I believed He had the tendency to show favoritism and be selective about who He allowed to be the recipient of His favor. Some religious folk love saying things like "favor ain't fair!" I knew that He is a God who requires holiness because He has given us the power to be so through the infilling of His Holy Spirit. (Following rules was never hard for me, so I had this down.) And, lastly, I understood God to desire closeness through prayer and Bible reading—things I didn't mind whatsoever, because I learned early on to read the Bible regularly. These are deeply problematic views of the God of the Bible for me, and my emptiness and the lack of experience with a father can be pointed to as a primary reason for this.

Over the years, I've tried to be very careful with blaming my deficits and traumas on the effects of father absence, while in the same breath I need to be reasonable so I can strike a careful balance. It's so easy to swing from one spectrum (the idea that I'm minimally affected by fatherlessness) to the other end of the spectrum (that everything wrong with my life and relationships is a result of fatherlessness). Sometimes, trying to discover specific ways I've been affected feels like I'm being weak and trying to find and place blame. It feels like I'm lacking the courage, fortitude, and mental toughness I've always had in order to overcome whatever challenges life threw my way. It makes me feel like I'm not willing to take responsibility for my life, and it chips away at the core I've developed within myself, which is to always be strong, endure, and pick myself up to push boldly ahead—no matter what.

But I've decided to let go of as many fears as I possibly can so I can begin moving forward. And to disregard the reality of the influence growing up without a father had on me, to dismiss or minimize its negative effects, does me—and everyone around me—a huge disservice. This reality and truth became even more apparent to me as I slowly recognized how my relationship with the Lord crossed over into my merely existing in a cycle where I was no longer growing and evolving within this relationship. My joy and excitement waned, and I was no longer responding internally to my religious habits and spiritual maneuvers. I experienced some serious valley seasons and grew pretty frustrated in my spirit, dissatisfied with the fruits of my faith and discouraged by my perception of God's presence in my day-to-day life.

Through my wrestling with God—as I attempted to see and relate to Him as my Father—my handicap helped me gain a much clearer understanding of how I'm impacted. I finally recognized how father absence laid the foundation for the majority of the empty pits in my life that, without a doubt, influenced the way I perceived everything and everyone around me. Especially the Lord. To be fair and comprehensive, my mother bears much responsibility as well. She did what she knew how and had the most direct hand in how I was molded and shaped. She gets the privilege of taking some of the credit for my good and great just as much as my bad and ugly. But I proudly take responsibility for it all. Which is the reason why learning to *live loved* is something I am being intentional with; living loved by my Heavenly Father is my current plight because it's something I wish I had the capacity to do a long time ago. This is so significant for me because, as a wife and mom, everything I am flows into my marriage and parenting, which will affect the generations to come. Living loved has to be a part of my legacy, and in order for that to happen, it has to be an authentic part of my everyday life.

Chapter 4

Abba Who?

We, society at large, should all know by now it's irrefutable that living life without a father is abnormal and detrimental to a child, and yet it remains the norm in many of our households and communities. In the same breath, I definitely see and hear about droves of men being intentional with being present in the lives of their children, regardless of the relationship status with their child(ren)'s mother. I don't have any statistics to back this up—and I can't say I'm even interested in finding out how things have and are shifting within our communities and across the nation—I'm only speaking from my limited sphere of experience and exposure. I am of the opinion that, at least in my generation, men know and understand life without a father, and many of them are adamant about not allowing that to be their legacy. But I still hesitated, wondering if it was worth sharing and talking about my own experience, considering how common fatherlessness remains.

I recognize the fact that in many homes the presence of a father can be just as detrimental as homes without, particularly in those instances where he is emotionally unavailable, yielding to substance abuse, violent, etc. I do not mean to paint the picture that homes with the presence of fathers are always full of smiles, birthday cakes, and Christmas year-round. I understand that there are some (or many) downsides to fathers who are in the home because of what their humanity, imperfections, sinfulness, and dysfunction present to their families. But I do see the ways in which the good of parents in reasonable situations will often outweigh the bad. For example, there are so many things throughout my life that my mother either got totally wrong or could have done so much better. I remember so many of her mistakes and things I'm sure she regrets—she's a sinful, dysfunctional woman who yielded on many occasions to her own humanity. As I do; as we all do. She had a tremendous amount of baggage, pain, and personal lack that she couldn't help but carry into her parenting. On top of that, she had to carry the burden of single motherhood and navigate the road of raising my brother and me at a very young age. Consequences of her own choices! But her reality, nevertheless. Despite everything—all her trials and hardships, mistakes, failures, and regrets—I will forever hold in my heart the good of my childhood and how it significantly outweighs the bad. Perhaps it's the resilience of children. Maybe it's the beautiful, unconditional love and longing that we will always have toward our parents who chose to stick it out and attempt to make the best of their circumstances. But I will always have a very genuine fondness for my mom and a significant level of appreciation for her efforts and sacrifices through the years. I imagine this has to be the same case with imperfect fathers in the home.

While writing this book, I made a Facebook post about Gerry's absence and how growing up without him was such a harsh reality. I compared how the absence of a father's presence, and not experiencing his authority and voice on a regular basis, affects all fatherless children in some way. An associate in my friends list disagreed with my perception of women like her who grew up with their fathers. She shared her opinion that my perception of women who grew up with their fathers was much more than reality. In so many words, she told me to stop thinking so highly of households like hers because the presence of their fathers isn't always what it's cracked up to be. When I read her comment, my immediate thought was, *That's her privilege speaking.*

A few weeks later, I saw her make a post with a picture of her and her father as she wished him a happy birthday and shared a few kind words about him. I smiled to myself and thought, *How ironic!* I completely understand that life for her wasn't perfect, even though she had her dad around. I have no idea what life was like for her or what kind of pain she could have been referencing that came as a result of her dad's failures, mistakes, and overall humanity. But after reading her Facebook post (I didn't care to comment because you never know what that could open), I became even more convinced that fathered women have more and do better in certain areas than those of us who grow up without fathers. They will have their own wounds and scars to heal from, but they also have a certain level of privilege that fatherless women will never have. And, unfortunately, fathered women will often be incapable of recognizing their privilege while minimizing and/or dismissing the pain and plight of the women who lack that privilege.

We've never experienced the simple things like having and experiencing our father's authoritative and masculine presence, hearing our father's voice on a regular basis. We didn't have the privilege of experiencing and learning (even if just through observation alone) the differences in how men reason, express themselves, and how they function and deal with circumstances—all of which are very different from women. We never had the pleasure of knowing and feeling what it is to belong and be accepted by a dad or experience his delight in us—the kind that only a dad can shower upon his offspring. It's easy to take these small and simple things for granted when it has been a regular part of our everyday lives. In fact, it's easy to disregard and dismiss how the lack of these things influences women who grew up without fathers, as my friend on Facebook demonstrated, not realizing that's what she was doing.

Male Presence on the Outskirts

I feel pretty strongly that having a consistent father figure in your life that replaces an absent father is a tremendous blessing. If there is a genuine father-child relationship cultivated and experienced through the years, that replacement—especially if it happens early enough—will prevent much of the emptiness, dysfunction, trauma, and baggage that comes with having no father around. Anything less than a genuine father-child relationship may be helpful in many ways, but a child will still have a nagging question surrounding why their biological father isn't around. Sometimes that nagging question remains, despite the blessing of having an exceptional stepfather or father figure. And in other instances, when the male in the home is not functioning as a father figure—he's just a male in the house enjoying the benefits of being in a relationship with the woman of the house—the lack of relationship between him and the child(ren) in the home renders his presence completely meaningless in the areas that matter most within a child's life. And that's not necessarily his fault, but I'm of the opinion that if you're going to be in a relationship with a person, living under the same roof where children reside, you've chosen to take on the responsibility of helping to parent those children. This choice should be evident when interacting with the child(ren) on some level.

I fall into the category where the male's presence was meaningless. My entire childhood was not spent completely absent of the presence of a male. My mother was (or became) a longterm-relationship kind of woman. Granted, I don't recall her having too many seasons of singleness, but I was a child and I certainly wasn't in tune with her love life, nor was I counting the months or years between her relationships. Of the long-term relationships I can remember, only one boyfriend lived with us, Mr. Billy, the gentleman who helped pull my family out of the projects. Despite his tenure under our roof, I remember very vividly the distance between him and me. My mom was hyper-sensitive when it came to the presence of men with little girls, and she made it a point to ensure there was an ocean-wide distance between me and any man she allowed in my presence, be it a boyfriend, uncle, family friend, neighbor, the neighbor's son, and so on. She didn't play! So even if a long-term boyfriend, uncle, or other male example had a genuine desire to take on the role of being a father figure to me, that genuine interest would have been intercepted by my mom in her quest to protect and preserve me. It was more important to her that she guaranteed I never had the innocence of my childhood yanked away versus letting me experience the love, balance, and affirmation that typically come with such a significant relationship.

So, as a child in relation to men, all I knew was distance and indifference. No adult male ever took a genuine interest in me (that I'm aware of); they couldn't care less about my likes and dislikes, my fears, insecurities, and joys. No adult male was concerned with helping me navigate life as a girl who would become a woman or taking responsibility for cultivating my character or facilitating my growth and development. This is why I find it exceedingly absurd to believe I could have the capacity to transition into a Father-daughter relationship with the Lord. How would I transition from the emptiness of being fatherless to existing and living life on this side of salvation *as a daughter of The King*? How do I begin to fathom a Father who is holy and perfect, full of grace and wisdom? How do I comprehend being the child of a Father whose love is consuming, sacrificial, and unconditional, and has limitless provision and protection?

Spiritual Transition

I was saved in 2002, which was my fourth year at SCSU. I was living alone in an apartment off campus that resembled the gray worn-out wooden, two-story house from the video "Thriller." It was literally that bad, minus the zombies and spiritual wickedness! At the time, I was casually seeing a guy in the military who was stationed in North Carolina, and his mother, who lived in Galveston, Texas, took an immediate interest in me—since I was involved with her son. During our first conversation over the phone, she asked me if I was saved, and I politely told her, "No, ma'am." She proceeded to ask me why not, and I was frank with her; I let her know that although I believed there was a God, I just wasn't so sure about this Jesus guy, and I didn't desire anyone's religion. I just wanted the truth. She and I chatted openly and often (every day almost), and it took no time for us to build a high level of trust within our budding relationship. After about thirty days, we were doing our usual chatting on the phone, probably about life, and the conversation shifted onto the topic of faith. I guess it was my time! I imagine the Holy Spirit had been hard at work softening my heart and helping me to open up during my daily conversations with Ms. Connie. While hanging out on my living room floor chatting with her, she asked if I wanted to allow Jesus Christ to enter my life and be my Lord. I don't remember why, but I was extremely emotional at this point, and I remember saying yes and repeated after Ms. Connie the prayer of salvation. Midway through my confession, I was in tears, and by the time we were done, I was curled up on the floor, sobbing. I remember hearing her praising the Lord, and not too long after, she said she was going to leave me to be ministered to by the Holy Spirit. At the time I didn't know what that meant, other than the fact I probably just needed to be alone, considering how emotional I was. But I'm glad she did. I don't recall how long the moment lasted, but it was beautiful to say the least.

Spiritually, I transitioned into a state of complete belonging. Within the blink of an eye, I was accepted and claimed, gaining access to the manifold blessings, privileges, and benefits that come along with sitting in this new position of having access to the Father through the blood of Jesus Christ. Not only did I have access to the Father, He also became *my* Father!

There's no way a person can shift, practically, from a life having the role of dad being vacant to a life where that role is newly filled. And this role in my life isn't just filled, it's filled to the point of overflowing! Within the faith, there is a constant reference to God as Father, so naturally I referred to Him as such, while never truly embracing—within the depth of my heart—the reality and significance of this new

Father-daughter relationship. To take it even deeper (at least for me), I've been on the receiving end of countless sermons and exhortations of folks using the term "Abba Father." In every instance throughout my years of salvation, this term of endearment—when referencing God—means absolutely nothing to me, even while intending to be a term oozing with meaning, substance, and relatability.

Intellectually, I understand the intention and sentiment behind its use. There's currently a debate surrounding the literal definition and primary meaning of the term Abba, but I have no interest in joining (or even following) this debate closely. Currently, I stand on the side of Abba being a reference to God that a child would use because of the intimacy and closeness of their relationship. In one of his devotionals, Brennan Manning says,

> In order to comprehend His [Jesus] relentless tenderness and passionate love for us, we must always return to His Abba experience. Jesus experienced God as tender and loving, courageous and kind, compassionate and forgiving, as laughter of the morning and comfort of the night. Abba, a colloquial form of address used by little Jewish children toward their fathers, and best translated "Papa" or "Daddy," opened the possibility of undreamed of, unheard of intimacy with God.[2]

This is my current understanding and acceptance of the term Abba, and the viewpoint I'm speaking from. Long story short, this has never been my experience with God! I've never had these thoughts or feelings toward Him, and because I still have yet to fully relate to God in this way, this Abba reference remains almost meaningless within my heart. This isn't my desire or intention; it's just my truth at this point in my relationship with Him.

---

2   Brennan Manning, "What Does it Mean to Call God Our 'Abba Father,'" NIV: New International Version (website), https://www.thenivbible.com/blog/god-our-abba-father/.

In fact, I've never taken the time until recently to consider what it means to be adopted into God's family through the saving grace of Jesus Christ. I operate within the supernatural realm pretty effectively since I have a solid understanding of the power and authority I possess when utilizing God's ministering spirits to intervene in the natural world or when engaging and standing against demonic influences. I know without a shadow of a doubt that this power and authority I possess is only made available to me because of my position as an adopted heir. Only now am I recognizing that there is (and has always been) another side of life as a believer that I've been missing out on. I share in more detail what I'm referring to in a later chapter, but walking around for years hearing and using the familial language we throw around in Christendom has helped perpetuate the emptiness of my dynamic with the Lord. I feel this is the case with many other believers within the body of Christ, too. For instance, titles such as "Sister So-and-So" and "Brother So-and-So" in some Christian traditions seem to have taken on a life of their own in the land of meaninglessness. This is an example of how something meant to be a sincere way of communicating with our spiritual family—since we are indeed spiritual siblings within the family of God—has become nothing more than an empty formality or title. Especially within those church traditions where titles are almost required whenever you're present within the four walls of a church building. I can find myself in the grocery store and see a member from church and sense the unwelcome feeling of addressing a person by their first name. And God forbid you refer to a leader of these traditional churches without their title! So, I've begun to take inventory of my language and which words concerning my faith actually mean something to me, and I find myself speculating on the degree to which other believers are carrying a similar type of emptiness—especially those who grew up without a father—when referencing God and declaring who He is. What percentage of Christians refer to God as *Father* or *Abba Father* and are genuinely speaking from an intimate experience from their Father-daughter or Father-son relationship?

Genuinely recognizing God as Lord of my life has served me tremendously well. In many ways, and at many times, I've experienced the wonders of who He is and how we benefit from belonging to Him. Many things within my relationship with God stretch significantly below the surface, are firmly planted, and have taken root in all the right places. I have been on the receiving end of proper and balanced spiritual nutrition throughout my life as a believer, and this is the primary reason why I've grown so solidly as a follower of Christ, capable of applying the Bible to my life in practical ways which enable me to thrive in *most* areas of my spiritual life.

Using Jesus' Parable of the Sower in Matthew 13, for example, much of me has been good soil in that I have a proper view and perspective of God being sovereign, eternal, transcendent, creator, and sustainer of all things. This has always produced a manifold crop, allowing me to be fruitful in the faith as I live it out on a day-to-day basis. But there has always been a level of relationship with the Lord that has evaded me. His character and virtues; His reputation, heart, feelings, and thoughts toward me; and His promises, blessings, and privileges that are extended to me—these are all intellectually understood through religion and my spiritual practices and habits. But these seeds of knowledge and truth, within the context of God being my Father, are those that fall among the thorns. They sprung up and began to choke my ability to live within the truth of God's fatherhood beyond my intellectual capacity.

When these two dynamics within me finally collided, my relationship with the Lord could no longer continue being sustained by the virtues that came from the good soil. The thorny side of me caused my overall progress to eventually come to a halt. No longer did I feel the same joy from my usual habits and routines. Reading my Bible, praying, worshipping, going to and serving in my local church, honoring God with my finances, and fellowship with others within the Body of Christ were no longer fulfilling or satisfying. Within my soul (being, my feeler, thinker, and chooser), what I had come to think and declare about my relationship with the Lord wasn't nearly as authentic or deeply rooted within my heart as it could have been. At least not by my standard. I hungered for significantly more and was able to recognize this when I came to grips with the reality that I didn't know, understand, nor honor God—let alone exist with Him—as my Father.

A Mangled Image

I came across an article online by Bill Gaultiere, a psychologist, author, and spiritual director for a ministry he and his wife formed called Soul Shepherding, where he talks about a number of believers who need healing within their image of the Lord. He mentioned that one of the ways we can determine whether we need healing in our image of God is by the way we answer a simple question: Can you look back over your whole life and say, "My Heavenly Father has always been good to me and truly mean it?" I've asked myself multiple times if I really believed in God's goodness within the depth of my heart, apart from my religious indoctrination and spiritual habits—neither of which are bad, per se. But each time I've posed that question to myself, my answer is primarily no, but with a yes in the background.

This is extremely complex for me. There is an enormous internal conflict that allows me, on one hand, to believe in the goodness of God because when I look back over the course of my life, especially since I've been saved, I see His hand. And it's incredible! However, I also see what I've interpreted as His failures regarding me, and these "failures" seem to be more etched in my soul. My perception of God's failures regarding me don't come close to outnumbering His goodness I've experienced, but they certainly outweigh it.

In my early years of cultivating my view and understanding of God, all the progress made became severely mangled because I dealt with another situation of sexual assault. This would be the second time, but this time, I was supposed to be within the protection of God! Not only that, I had begun the work of allowing the Holy Spirit to work on my temperament—my outlook on life and people, my personality, character, and natural inclinations. My view was I had to let go of all the things I had created around myself to prevent abuse from happening again. This assault was nothing close to the first time, and my course of action was very different (I didn't suffer in silence, I reported the incident to the police, etc.), but it was still very traumatic, and it packed a severe blow to my image of God because it happened at a time when I was a babe in Him. I liken this time to the life stage of a human baby and all the ways a baby is dependent on the caregiver, especially when it comes to being protected.

My view of the Lord's failure, and the loss of faith and trust I experienced toward Him, is not something I can describe. And while all this was taking place inside me, I somehow managed to be good soil when it came to seeing God from a particular vantage point that allowed me to operate effectively (most times) within the spiritual realm. While at the same time, grappling with Him regarding a different vantage point that didn't at all paint Him in a positive light.

Truth in the inward parts has always been something I possessed, although in a secular sense, prior to salvation. So, recognizing the truth about how I feel and what I believe about God isn't complicated and has always flowed freely within our dynamic. For instance, when I praise and worship through song, I'll either change the lyrics that don't accurately capture how I truly feel about Him, or I'll hum certain sections of a song that don't depict what I genuinely think about Him. These are definitely moments where my emotions kick into high gear to the point of tears because I have that conflict again—I feel bad that the posture in my heart toward the Lord isn't what I believe He deserves, while at the same time, recognizing the reason for this is because I don't completely believe He's deserving! Being honest with myself and transparent with Him allows me to be vulnerable, while preventing me from being self-deceived about my reality. I don't let empty declarations about the Lord fly through my lips, except on those occasions where I am working to shift something within my life (or the life of others) that requires me to speak boldly and audibly into the atmosphere. There's a specific intention in these instances, but other than that, I refuse to speak the language of Christendom and all the clichés that come from being immersed in church culture. I've just grown very tired of it, especially in an era where folks are becoming more culturally Christian and churched, rather than genuine followers of Christ, living out His example both publicly and privately.

I have moments where I feel saddened, maybe even ashamed, that I don't have a solid yes to Bill Gaultiere's question in my heart. Not being able to refer to Him as Abba Father actually bothers me; I desire to be fathered by Him and I long to capitalize on and take advantage of all that's supposed to be available to me as His child. It's important that my Abba reference carries with it what Jesus experienced as I dare to hope that I'll be able to grasp for myself this same experience with the Father. I don't know to what degree this is realistic, but I'm willing to have a heart open enough to give us a chance!

While listening to a Focus on the Family broadcast, the person being interviewed expressed the idea that an earthly father's humanity should not define fatherhood and everything that encompasses fatherhood. God has already defined fatherhood with being the original Father of all; and while this may be true, how do I travel to this truth so that I can own it for myself? How do I navigate to this reality, practically, when I have no reference point from which to launch myself?

When discussing the need for our image of God to be healed, Gaultiere notes that people like me need to shift how we compare earthly fathers and their fatherhood to that of the Lord's. God is the literal Father, while earthly fathers can have many similarities and attributes. Not the other way around. God is often compared to earthly fathers (which I've made the mistake of doing), when in reality earthly fathers and their fatherhood should be compared to, or measured against, the standard God has already exemplified and set.

I really appreciate this perspective because of how it's redirecting my attention and focus away from the failures of an earthly father by pointing me toward the perfection and standard of my Heavenly Father. Gerry was the bridge that would, at the very least, land me on the other side so I could, at some point, be capable of navigating to God's throne. This bridge I required had collapsed before I reached my second birthday, and with all sincerity, I asked the Lord, "How do I begin my journey toward You?" His answer was simple, as He pointed me to Romans 12:2 (NIV, emphasis mine):

> Do not conform to the pattern of this world,
> but *be transformed by the renewing of your mind.*
> Then you will be able to test and approve what
> God's will is—his good, pleasing and perfect will.

To say the least, I was unexcited and uninspired. How was I supposed to do this? How and where would I even begin? I need for things to be plain, practical, and preferably include steps—and a few instructions! The Lord's way of solving my dilemma was folded a few times, under layers; however, this was my starting point, which was intended to allow the Holy Spirit to redefine and reshape my understanding of fatherhood through the Scriptures. He simply wanted me to be intentional with meditating on the different verses He would bring to my attention. He got my attention by causing something within me to stir when I came across these different verses. (I talk about this in detail later and share how God reinforced this process.) This facilitated my transformation through the rebuilding of the collapsed bridge that was preventing me from getting closer to Him.

Quiet Time with the Lord (Journal Entries)

November 21, 2018 - 2:39 p.m.

Abba Father means nothing to me. It doesn't resonate with me in the least. Perhaps part of that has to do with the fact that I'm a child born in the 21st century in the Western world, immersed in Western culture. But even in its intended use, the translation doesn't do anything for me.

December 20, 2018 - 11:00 p.m.

I just got out of the shower, and after a series of thoughts, I found myself in tears as I shared with God how I don't have feelings or believe that I am exceedingly cherished by Him. I have been studying lately the culture of women in the Bible in ancient Israel and how they seem to be mistreated and marginalized. And with it being the Word of God, I just felt like He likely doesn't place a huge value on women because he made Adam first, making Eve second, and throughout the history of the ancient Israelites, women were not treated equally and they were not seen as equals even though there are references that seem to point to there being a high value placed on us. And, so, I was very tearful as I was sharing with Him how sorry I am that I'm not able to feel His love, to feel like I'm cherished or worthy, to feel like I mean so much more to Him. I feel sorry that I don't really trust Him anymore; I feel sorry that I don't really believe everything that I could and should believe as it relates to His character and His feelings and thoughts toward me. I don't feel like being a daughter to Him is as important and as valued as being a son would. And, unfortunately, it feels as though the Word of God doesn't really do a good job of debunking any of the feelings I have because it seems to reiterate how men have treated women and how men felt about women. And the fact that this is reflected in the Bible is just not helpful. In fact, it's more damaging.

So, as I begin to listen to the Lord talk to me, it feels as though He's telling me that it's okay that I feel the way that I feel. He's telling me that I am on a journey, and it's His job to get me to my destination. I was beginning to share how I hate the fact that it feels like I have to work; I have to put forth effort and energy into learning how to feel loved by Him as opposed to Him doing all the work—because, honestly, I don't feel like it's my fault that I'm here in the first place. It's not of my doing that I feel this way or am unable to feel the way I probably should as it relates to being his child/daughter. I just feel like being the daughter of the King, being the daughter of a Father who sits in Heaven, should mean something so significant. But right now, it just doesn't feel like it means anything. And I just really hope this changes.

Chapter 5

Healing is a Choice

Simply put, healing from and overcoming different types of trauma and their psychological impact requires a high level of consistent and intentional energy and effort over the course of time. The time it takes is unique to us individually and highly depends on the choices we make throughout the process. The level of healing depends on the amount of work we put forth and the resources around us we choose to tap into and embrace. Without a shadow of a doubt, I believe that virtually all situations and circumstances placed before me will offer a minimum of two options, despite my willingness or ability to recognize these options. I can either 1) choose to heal and journey through the process, or 2) do nothing and remain the person I have been—grappling with the same cycles of thoughts, emotions, and issues that will continue to reverberate beneath the surface, regardless of how well I learn to cope as the years progress.

I've seen the latter often. In fact, I'm close to quite a few people who have chosen to take that route, and I loathe the idea of being numbered among those who choose to do nothing. I hate the idea of carrying on with life as usual while I continue to manage day to day with my usual dysfunctional ways of thinking, reacting internally, coping, and responding externally—only to live with the consequences. The stunted growth and slow, misinformed learning, or progress, that takes place in these situations are painful to observe. The discomfort of intentionally shifting in the areas we need for change and healing to take place—and the fear of the unknown behind the door of change—is perceived as being a bit too much. So, it becomes too costly and not worth moving on because our perception is our reality.

It doesn't feel good to hear, but doing nothing and carrying on with life and business as usual is ultimately the choice to reject healing, wholeness, and restoration. It's the choice to continue trudging through the sewage of our lives, carrying the emotional burdens and baggage that melt into our temperament and flow freely through the channels of our thoughts and the veins of our behavior. And because we know no other way to exist and walk through life, we settle into this bondage, making our dysfunctions our norm. Our internal dysfunctions are like the towns on the outskirts where we've chosen to settle in and thereby exist comfortably uncomfortable, while still living on the outskirts of what life can and should be: full, abundant, joyous, and worth living.

Every healed and delivered individual I've ever encountered, either directly or indirectly, made the deliberate choice to be so. And rarely is this choice an easy one to make. What I find peculiar is the fact we all desire, even if just on the surface, what we know to be in our best interest. We all want what will benefit us, while in the same breath, the deeper the trauma and pain, the easier it is to remain sitting comfortably uncomfortable in the seat of our dysfunction. Again, the perception of the pain, the discomfort of change, and the fear of the unknown work against us, helping us remain defeated and immobile.

The process of arriving at the place where I chose healing and restoration took a lot of effort, only to find it merely put me in the position to now embark on the *actual* journey of being healed, which is significantly more work. It took a tremendous amount of courage and energy to examine, through the lens of truth, my life and relationships. It took an extraordinary amount of self-reflection and effort to dig up and explore my past, especially where there has been mental, physical, and emotional abuse and trauma. It's easy to be convinced that it's in our best interest to leave the past behind us and to allow the suppressed or lost memories to remain in the abyss. However, leaving the past in the past is almost never beneficial; no matter how much we want to believe we have the ability to do so, a past not addressed and dealt with is always with us, constantly informing the way we see and live life. As far as I'm concerned, there is no such thing as moving on with life in a way that's healthy, functional, and normal while having a history of trauma, wounds, and scars left unaddressed. If I were to believe this, I'm deceiving myself into remaining paralyzed within my oppression.

Father absence planted seeds, which over time, sprouted into a jungle—placed smack in the middle of the forest of life. The added learning curve, complications, and hurdles made life significantly more difficult to maneuver once the trauma and suffering from rape were piled on. It's as if I was already at a disadvantage at the beginning of the race. The last thing my battered soul wanted to do was take time to examine and possibly relive the circumstances that inflicted the agony I was living with, deep beneath the surface. Who in their right mind has any desire to reflect on the circumstances surrounding any form of neglect or abuse experienced—or the perpetrator(s) that sit at the center of this mental and emotional suffering?

Nevertheless, this is the very step I had to take to begin my journey of healing and being made whole. This was the prerequisite for beginning my trek down the road of learning how to live loved. After I embraced the reality that my journey required the painful examination of my past, I delayed the choice to move forward. The fear and pain were incredibly difficult. Climbing out of the valley only to relive some of the most painful aspects of my past caused a few years' delay. I absolutely didn't want to remain in my dysfunction, or within the norm trauma had created for me, but it was easier to remain in the comfort of what had become my reality. Again, I found myself sitting comfortably uncomfortable in my own little town, right on the outskirts of the city where everything life could and should have been for me during that season of my life.

And that was a choice.

Unexpected Catalyst

It wasn't until I was amid a painful conflict with an individual (a man) who had a level of spiritual authority and leadership over me that I had finally had enough. I was thrust into the position of choosing whether I would continue to allow cowardice and avoidance to keep me bound while I continued having the same misunderstandings and made the same mistakes but with different people. As a more seasoned believer, I can now say it came down to being willing to put faith into action while learning to trust God and His ability to shoulder the burden I had been carrying around for so many years.

The catalyst that set things in motion was strife between me and the previous leadership at my church. My husband and I were pretty close to another married couple in the church, along with our pastor and his girlfriend at the time (now his wife). The six of us hung out together, especially after Sunday morning worship service, and we became pretty good friends. As we spent more time together and grew closer, as with all relationships, disagreements and conflict arose. Unfortunately, we didn't have the maturity or ability as a group (or as individuals) to resolve these conflicts appropriately or effectively, despite how spiritual we were.

At one point, I felt my pastor didn't quite understand or know how to operate within the boundaries of our friendships and his pastoral leadership over us, but particularly as it related to me. I sometimes felt like I was the black sheep of the group because I was very vocal about my convictions and positions, especially when they differed from anyone else within the group. I didn't have the grace or the peaceable spirit necessary in the company of others who were just as convinced about their viewpoint. To be quiet or hold my peace when my position is different from someone else's equates to one of two things: either my silence shows agreement or my silence is permission for people to be wrong. Now add onto that the abrasive nature I had back then!

Eventually I felt both mistreated and mishandled by my pastor, and while venting to a close friend (also within the pastorate), I was reminded of how I began seeing a Christian counselor years prior in hopes of resolving my issues of fatherlessness. My friend listened to the details surrounding my conflict with my pastor and pieced together things that pointed to my expectations, vulnerabilities, and even wounds that either remained open or were being reopened as a result of my conflict with a man who had a type of authority within my life. *The irony*, I thought.

I was very appreciative of his sensitivity and honesty. He admonished me to pursue counseling again, and after spending a moment in prayer, the Lord took no time in leading me to a Christian counselor that I immediately reached out to. I made up my mind and decided it was time to just go on and tackle everything I had been spending years avoiding. There is nothing like a made-up mind!

Arriving at my first counseling session, and during our discussion, my counselor discerned that before we would get into the effects of fatherlessness, I needed to receive deliverance and healing from the impact and trauma of being sexually assaulted. The first assault was such an overwhelming burden to carry around on so many different levels, to the degree that I attempted to take my own life. However, the second time I was assaulted had a much different and oppressive effect because it occurred soon after I had become saved and as we say in the church, "on fire for the Lord!" At the time, I was thoroughly enjoying my membership at my first church, Greater Mt. Calvary Holy Church in Northeast DC, despite it being a mega church. I was very active and plugged in, especially since there were so many ministries at my disposal, from the Mime Ministry to attending classes at the church's Calvary Bible Institute. I was experiencing the presence of the Holy Spirit in such profound and undeniable ways, and on a regular basis. As I've shared, my faith walk and new life as a believer began cultivating drastic changes in my temperament, my standards, my behaviors, and the overall way I viewed life. This season was absolutely amazing! So, to be in a position where I would experience being sexually assaulted *again*, and then for it to happen on what felt like God's watch, was . . . unspeakable. This is precisely what my counselor wanted me to address first because it shattered my relationship with the Lord, and this new series of hang-ups that emerged and began running in the background of my life required my immediate attention. There was no way I'd be able to allow the Holy Spirit to redefine and reshape my understanding of His fatherhood while I still bled a level of blame that I felt *He* needed to own for "allowing" me to be sexually assaulted. Especially at a time when I supposedly belonged to Him! I didn't carry any blame in my heart toward the Lord for the first assault because I blamed myself and believed—since I hadn't yet accepted Him as Lord—I didn't belong to Him at that point in my life. But I was required to first get over the obstacle of both assaults in order to begin the work of addressing any daddy issues.

So, when my counselor informed me that dealing with the sexual trauma was the greater priority and that issues surrounding fatherlessness would need to take a back seat, I was dismayed. I remember sitting on her couch looking at the floor, trying to process what she was telling me, all the while trying to control and suppress the different emotions bubbling up. Finally, I had a mind that was made up and had arrived at the place where I was ready to plunge into what I was certain had always been the primary issue spilling out and polluting every area of my life—only to have to be diverted and hurled down a different path. One I never intended traveling down. Now looking back, it's ironic, maybe even weird, that it never occurred to me that being raped was something I'd need to address! Those were two instances I somehow managed to live with, as if it didn't really affect me. It was just a part of my past, a history I had accepted for what it was and moved on from. I don't even remember sharing with my counselor anything about those instances during that initial session, which in some ways speaks to how "normal" it was to have experienced such an ordeal—on two different occasions, at that—and how I believed I was living life like any other typical person. But I do remember the halting moment within our discussion where she shared her thoughts on how we would be reprioritizing the topic of our future sessions. I remember the jolt I felt inside and the pause that left me staring down at her floor.

With my saved, sanctified, Holy Ghost-filled self, how did I allow myself to push those instances into the furthest recesses of my mind, to the degree that I couldn't recognize the level of damage I was walking around with? With my seasoned self, how was I missing the reality that my relationship with the Lord was deteriorating moment by moment over the years? And deteriorating not only because of my daddy issues but also due to harboring feelings and thoughts toward Him regarding past trauma I believe He could have found a way to prevent. The past trauma alone kept Him confined to a space in my soul that allowed me to be the judge and jury. When it came to matters of my heart, the Lord and His Word sometimes had very little influence. Nonetheless, God, through my counselor, saw the urgency of addressing my spiritual condition, but beyond what I felt was being brought to the table. He just needed to get me to the table. Spiritually, I was walking around with two rotten and decomposing bodies tied to my back, and the Lord decided which of the two would be removed first and buried appropriately.

Breakthrough

Having finally made the choice to pursue healing handed me the victory over one of the most difficult parts of the war. That choice was the reason why I was finally sitting on her couch. But I sat there paralyzed for a moment because discussing those extremely humiliating events, unearthing the devastation, and sifting through and then reconciling the psychological effects of being twice assaulted, was territory I wasn't prepared to cover. This pivot being sprung on me so suddenly, was necessary because I didn't have time to deliberate long, and I wasn't alone during the moments I did have. I don't know if she was watching me, but she sat peacefully quiet in her chair possibly praying for me, giving me the space I needed. But this setup is what prevented me from regressing into yet another delay that could have lasted a few more months, or years even. The Lord was very strategic in making sure He helped me move forward by capitalizing on a made-up mind and the presence of one of His vessels.

With the small amount of time I had to consider this new commitment, I looked up from the floor and made eye contact with my counselor and nodded with a shrug, agreeing to move forward. Within what felt like a split second, I chose to trust God knew what He was doing and decided it was okay for once to not be the one in control; I was willing to press on the brake, put my car in park, and let go of the wheel to allow Him to take over per His wisdom and will.

After about six months of working through the counseling sessions and a workbook, I received my first significant breakthrough. To say the least, I put forth an unimaginable amount of heart and effort into the process of healing. I remember departing from work an hour or so early for each of my sessions and always had an extra pep in my step when making my way to her office! Working through my workbook pushed and pulled on me in ways and in directions I could have never imagined. It forced me to dig deeper than I thought I was capable of, and I had sessions where I cried to the point of not being able to talk for minutes at a time. But I never left a session heavy; I always felt lighter in my soul, and as my perspective was shifting, the perpetual storm clouds hovering over me finally began to part. I don't remember ever dreading any of my counseling sessions and the time I spent progressing through the things that had my soul so deeply entangled. Now, I *did* have moments where I dreaded working through that workbook! But I pushed forward because I needed to and had made the commitment.

As I experienced the intangible taking place within the deepest parts of me, my life was changing, and the lens through which I perceived life, love, relationships, conflict, and most importantly, the Lord Himself, became progressively clearer. And I would do it all over again in a heartbeat. The delay of this process is a huge mistake I would love to regret, but I can't afford to live there; I prefer to simply exist in the gratefulness I have toward the Lord for His nudges that pushed me forward in the direction He knew I needed to travel.

Chapter 6

Fatherhood Redefined

As I progress through the writing of this book, the Lord is redefining my perspective of fatherhood. I haven't arrived yet. My understanding of what it is to be fathered is continually being reshaped as I move through life and its seasons—singleness, married life, and now motherhood; abundance, lack, just enough; career woman, unemployed, entrepreneur, and stay-at-home mom; and so on. I enjoy seeing my progress and how I'm moving through each season because of intentionality. I'm constantly looking for and expecting to see and experience the fruit of my endeavor to live loved; and seeing God's hand and how He's working in me is such a joy to experience.

I'm glad I finally got to this point, because I was not originally excited about venturing into the Bible to begin the process of being "transformed by the renewing of my mind." Scripture can be so easy to pull from for answers, clarity, and guidance, but other times I really dislike sifting through the Bible because it can be so daunting. It sometimes feels like a lifetime to receive the Holy Spirit's revelation about a matter, and this is coming from an avid reader and lover of God's Word! I just had to bite the bullet and stay committed to trusting Him and allowing Him to guide, inform, and reveal His truth as He sees fit.

"I will be a Father to you, and you will be my sons and daughters, says the Lord Almighty."
(2 Cor 6:18)

To Come from Him

My endeavor began with my favorite Scripture—Psalm 139.

You have searched me, Lord, and you know me.
You know when I sit and when I rise;
you perceive my thoughts from afar.
You discern my going out and my lying down;
you are familiar with all my ways.
Before a word is on my tongue,
you, Lord, know it completely.
You hem me in behind and before,
and you lay your hand upon me.
Such knowledge is too wonderful for me,
too lofty for me to attain.
Where can I go from your Spirit?
Where can I flee from your presence?
If I go up to the heavens, you are there;
if I make my bed in the depths, you are there.
If I rise on the wings of the dawn,
if I settle on the far side of the sea,
even there your hand will guide me,
your right hand will hold me fast.
If I say, "Surely the darkness will hide me
and the light become night around me,"
even the darkness will not be dark to you;
the night will shine like the day,
for darkness is as light to you.
For you created my inmost being;
you knit me together in my mother's womb.
I praise you because I am fearfully and wonderfully made;
your works are wonderful,
I know that full well.

My frame was not hidden from you
when I was made in the secret place,
when I was woven together in the depths of the earth.
Your eyes saw my unformed body;
all the days ordained for me were written in
your book before one of them came to be.
How precious to me are your thoughts, God!
How vast is the sum of them!
Were I to count them, they would outnumber the grains
of sand—when I awake, I am still with you.[3]

When I came across Psalm 139 for the first time, it melted my heart in many ways because I encountered the knowledge of God concerning little ol' me. His knowledge of me attempted to communicate to my heart the possibility that His interest in me was intense, passionate, and consuming, which was something I had never experienced from a man before. Although this has always been my all-time favorite Scripture (the whole chapter!), it took a few years for me to finally begin believing in my heart—beyond God's *ability* to know all these things—He *desires* to be meticulously aware of all things concerning me. He is genuinely consumed with *me*.

I still have some road left to travel down when it comes to embracing this truth completely in my heart, but I've made considerable progress. In my mind, it takes nothing for the Lord to know everything; He's an omniscient being. So, it's easy to believe what He's capable of, I just have to embrace and begin believing the other side, the part where He's genuinely consumed with knowing me *because it's His desire*. But, at the very least, as a mom, I have a glimpse into how His knowledge of me on such a molecular level confirms that I do come from Him. I can grasp the concept that coming from Him is a large part of the reason why He

---

3   Psalm 139:1–18.

is consumed and has a vested interest in me, because that's how I relate to my boys. I am consumed with knowing them, and I spend a considerable amount of time observing and learning them. I am extremely vested, and I want to know everything!

To say that my heart was starving for this reality is such an understatement. To have someone as significant as God make the pronouncement that I come from Him, belong to Him, and that His knowledge of me is far above and beyond what any earthly being can ever fathom about me is such a game changer—as I *allow* it to take root in my heart. Most believers love declaring how we (mankind) are made in the likeness and image of God and that He breathed His essence into us, the breath of life (Gen 1:26 and 2:7). I dare say that more than a biological father, I'm from God and I'm fully accepted by Him through the blood and redemption of Jesus Christ. And this has always been the case, despite my being unaware of it throughout my life. Comprehending this intellectually is one thing—I've long accepted these truths in my mind—but to have a heart open enough to receive these truths on a much deeper level is a completely different situation. I've transitioned to embracing this reality and the idea that the Lord is always looking at me, surrounding me, and is keenly aware of me because of *His* internal desire and longing to do so. But I had to take responsibility and choose to believe this. Making these types of choices isn't easy because life has a way of competing with me, and I don't always win. The battlefield of my mind has such formidable opponents because I've lived with my old perceptions and beliefs for so long. Everything in me that opposes God—and His truths found throughout Scripture—has a tremendous pull on my mind and heart because I've lived much longer in my state of brokenness than I have in a state of being healed and emotionally whole. Not only am I exercising spiritual muscles I have never used before, I'm also experiencing unfamiliar emotions as I try to shift from living life as a believer who sees myself primarily as God's servant and slave to seeing myself as His beloved and child.

I recognized my servant and slave mentality while reading *Rediscovering the Kingdom* by Myles Munroe,[4] where he talks about God's original plan for mankind. My interpretation of what he outlined includes the differences between God's original plan and intention for us versus religion's plan and intention. Pulling two examples from his book, God wants a

- family of spirit sons and daughters—but religion wants servants and subjects
- relationship with men and women—but religion wants religion[5]

He goes on to describe the vast differences between the privileges and rights of sons and daughters versus servants and slaves and states,

> Jesus said that sons [and daughters] are members of the family, but servants are not. From the beginning, God wanted offspring who would relate to Him in love, not slaves or "hired hands" who would obey Him out of obligation. Servants may relate to their master on a superficial level, but no intimacy or sense of family exists. Sons [and daughters], on the other hand, are part of the family; they are heirs who will inherit everything that belongs to their father.[6]

Munroe explains that although a king has subjects (individuals who are "subject" to his rule), they are never considered to be in the same class or to carry the status of royalty. Although God is King, He doesn't want subjects! He wants sons and daughters who are entitled to carry the status of royalty and operate within those privileges. Reading his book was the first time I really understood the disconnect I have between my understanding of democracy, and our way of life, to that of a monarchy—when the Bible makes references to a king and his kingship, kingdom,

---

4   Myles Munroe, *Rediscovering the Kingdom* (Shippensburg: Destiny Image Publishers, Inc., 2004).

5   Ibid., p. 38.

6   Ibid., p. 39.

rule, authority, etc. All I know is the American and Westernized way of life and worldview; I have no real knowledge or understanding of monarchies and how they operate. For the majority of my life as a believer, I've been primarily God's servant, embracing the ideology from Apostle Paul, for example, who considered himself a slave of the Gospel, in chains for the cause of Christ. Granted, Paul is a little extreme for my taste, and it's been a challenge adopting his philosophy, since he was literally in chains, but I understand it! And I recognize the concept of being a servant of God. And being His slave isn't necessarily negative. These concepts are discussed throughout the New Testament, and they don't negatively affect me. It's just, in my instance, being a slave and a servant carried more weight than being a child.

Reading this section in Munroe's book really opened my eyes. Through the years, I experienced many moments where I was able to tap into the love of God, His favor, blessings, and all those other wonderful things, but I never really related to Him as more than His subject. I've spent a significant amount of time either trying to be worthy of everything that's freely available or to work to earn my inheritance, all the while fully understanding the doctrine of the Bible and my gross inability to do either. Intellectually, I have sound doctrine in me. But emotionally and psychologically, biblical doctrine has taken a back seat because of my emptiness and brokenness.

Like practicing God's presence, I'm practicing allowing myself to be who I am—His beloved. I'm practicing believing in my heart that I come from the Lord and belong to Him. In fact, I've even created a definition for my name Delmesha: "Beloved of the Sovereign Lord." And yes, I literally just made that up and decided it's the meaning behind my name because who's going to check me!

A Father's Provision

Over the years, I've come across the viewpoint prevalent in most cultures that the husband is the one with the primary responsibility of providing for his household. I've totally bought into and live out this philosophy myself as a stay-at-home mom. (Sidebar: let me just say that there is absolutely no debate about gender roles and whether women should work outside the home and have careers. Do you!!) However, prior to becoming a wife and mom, I experienced the provision of the Lord during my seasons of unemployment, through my own hands as I worked and climbed the corporate ladder in IT, and as I endeavored in my entrepreneurial ventures. I now have the blessing of experiencing the Lord's provision primarily through the hands and skills of my husband. I easily understand the concept of God providing for me in different seasons—as I've always understood God as my provider. Religion has made sure I understood this. I've viewed God as my provider purely because 1) He is God and 2) I'm a believer. Rarely, if ever, does it cross my mind, let alone penetrate my heart, that He has always been providing for me *because He is my Father.*

There are many verses in the Bible that resonate with me regarding God and His provision, but Matthew 6:8 speaks to my heart the most.

"Therefore, do not be like them [hypocrites and heathens]. For your Father knows the things you have need of before you ask Him."

For years, I have chosen to believe that God provides for me, so this is almost a cakewalk. I just have to choose to see His hand of provision through the lens of His simply being my Father and try to embrace the idea that He takes tremendous pleasure, pride, and joy in fulfilling the role of provider—and He takes this responsibility very seriously. I have the privilege of receiving small glimpses of this through my husband. Every now and then, the Holy Spirit speaks to me when I watch my husband provide for his children. I'm learning to treasure these glimpses because they deposit in me confidence and a sense of security as I develop and grow within my Father-daughter dynamic with the Lord.

But I still find myself wrestling with the Lord during those times when financial troubles hit. I would love to be completely stable in this area, but to be honest, I can shift like the waves of the sea. I know God is able, but sometimes I question if He's willing. It's nothing to regurgitate Philippians 4:19, "God shall supply all of my needs according to His riches in glory," but that verse can sometimes feel too lofty. Other times it feels completely empty, and other times it's exactly what I need to encourage my heart when having financial difficulty (not that this verse is limited to financial provision, but that's when it's referred to the most). It's easy to fall into existing day to day, not actually looking to the Lord to supply any need that arises. There's great wisdom and common sense in relying on my own resourcefulness, skills, experience, and gifts, but I'm trying to do better at balancing all that by first leaning and relying on an invisible God. Depending on where my mind is and what season of life I find myself, striking this balance is such a challenge. When things don't happen when or how I feel they should, despite my understanding of how God intervenes on the earth, I can easily lose sight of my authority on the earth as a believer and totally neglect to utilize the power of God's Word, filtered through faith. I've always understood my position as a believer and how to operate in the supernatural realm, but I never recognized why I had this position in the first place; I never filtered these privileges through my position as the child of the King. I've had long seasons where I stood on God's Word in a way that yielded significant, and even miraculous, results. But every now and then, I fall "off the wagon," and sometimes these off-the-wagon moments last for weeks, even months. This probably happens because I've never allowed myself to experience the full breadth of God's provision as His daughter, but also because of my humanity and natural inclination to do things all wrong! But at least I now recognize where my opportunities lie during this shifting of my perspective in the area of provision.

A Father's Discipline

Books, articles, and podcasts on parenting love to express the sentiment that although children don't like being disciplined, being corrected by their parents for wayward behavior fosters security and communicates they are loved. To be frank, this doesn't seem anywhere near the reasoning of a child, whether consciously or subconsciously. But that's just me! I just can't imagine my children ever truly understanding within themselves the idea that Mommy and Daddy's love is the reason and motivation behind forbidding them from having or doing something they want. Granted, they will hopefully come to this truth as they mature, but only when and if we communicate this principle and truth through the years. But even then, I'm not sure if this is something a child will grasp when even adults fail to grasp this concept.

Many times I've experienced how exceptional God's style of parenting is and how beautifully He disciplines and corrects, especially after He pricks my heart when I'm doing it all wrong with my boys! The fact of the matter is I only know what I know. But being filled with the Holy Spirit has allowed me to experience the gentle conviction that informs me of how my dysfunction has been spilling over into my parenting. Within this last year, I've been very purposeful in leaning on Him to correct and guide me in this area. I can't fathom my own children being damaged or even traumatized, having to spend precious years of their adulthood trying to unravel and heal from the dysfunctions of their mother. In some instances, that's just the way the cookie crumbles. But I have a choice in the matter when it comes to *my* legacy. I've chosen not to use their built-in resilience as my own personal buffer. I don't want to be idealistic; I refuse to rely on the notion that they will still "turn out okay" despite me. It's too easy to resort to the idea that since we turned out okay, they will too. They deserve better than that. And besides, who's to say we turned out okay? God has placed wonderful moms around me, some with very different temperaments that I can glean from, and in addition to that, I've been reading quite a few devotionals specifically on the topic of parenting from a Christian worldview. The progress I've made in my parenting has been beautiful, and it all started when I was disciplining my almost four-year-old. I looked into his eyes and immediately felt in my heart, *He deserves so much better . . . even though he was wrong and out of line.* There's nothing wrong with correcting and disciplining. It's necessary. It's the *way* it's done that matters.

> "My son [daughter], do not make light of the Lord's discipline, and do not lose heart when He rebukes you, because the Lord disciplines the one He loves, and He chastens everyone He accepts as His son [daughter]." (Heb 12:5b–6, *addition of daughter mine*)

Recognizing how important it is for the Lord to administer His discipline and correction is easy. I understand that His intended purpose is to shape my overall character, cause me to develop different virtues, shift my perspective on life and how to live it, etc. These things are easy for me to understand. But my understanding of God's discipline primarily comes through the filter of legalism and servitude, not from being His child.

Ensuring I didn't mess things up while serving Him was the primary way I understood God's overarching purpose for disciplining us. I always believed that what mattered most to Him was that I never dishonor His name or tarnish His reputation, which would ultimately bring shame to the body of Christ and disgrace the ministry I'm supposed to be representing on His behalf. Whenever God was disappointed with me and decided to discipline or correct, I don't think it ever crossed my mind that it had everything to do with His love for me. Perhaps this came about through how I interpreted and internalized the preaching and teaching I've sat under through the years, coupled with my own perceptions, resulting from my own childhood. I don't know. But even as an adult who clearly understands the principle that good parents discipline and correct out of love, God's correction originating out of His love for me hasn't completely penetrated my heart—and it hasn't been anything I believed beyond my intellect.

Because my heart is now more opened than ever, and because I'm especially sensitive in the area of parenting at the moment, I'm able to recognize the gentleness of the Lord's discipline; I'm beginning to feel how delicate He is when He chooses to correct or redirect me. I wish I could recall the circumstances, but what I do remember, and very vividly, is feeling the Holy Spirit chastising and correcting me while I was smack dab in the middle of my error. I could literally hear and feel the gentleness in His voice. I felt His love when He questioned me, redirecting me from whatever I was either doing or contemplating doing. I felt His kindness and compassion in His tone, and His words were laced with complete understanding. Picture the Lord sitting on the side of the bed with me, His hand resting on the small of my back while He shared the truth of my situation and His preferred way for me to move forward. It was a situation where, because of how He responded to me and the way He was dealing with me, I had no choice but to melt into His truth and relax in His love. There was no other way to respond! Accepting and embracing what He shared came with such ease, and turning in the direction He was pointing toward took very little thought or effort. This is my greatest experience—and only example—of exceptional parenting and correction that was truly through the filter of wisdom, understanding, love, and gentleness. And this example served me up a double-edged reminder of 1) His character, while 2) showing me just how much I fail at this high level of parenting with my own boys. Fortunately, the latter no longer comes with a healthy dose of shame or embarrassment; it's just the plain old truth. But it's becoming easier to embrace since I've been intentional with maturing and developing as a mom.

At times, remembering the feeling of being at peace after being corrected by the Lord can take some effort for me. I have to be deliberate in choosing to see and feel God's understanding, wisdom, and love in His correction. I can only relate on a very small scale because although I love my children very deeply and have grown tremendously in my parenting style, I still often fail to wrap my discipline and correction in the paper of love, understanding, compassion, and gentleness these kids deserve. I've had the habit of dipping way down into my humanity when I'm in the trenches with my boys, because that's what I experienced growing up. This is on top of my personal issues and dysfunctions; so attributing these characteristics and dysfunctions to the fatherhood of the Lord makes perfect sense. It's wrong, ineffective, and unproductive, but it makes sense that I would operate contrary to His way.

I can definitely see God's purpose, and I'm able to experience His heart when He corrects, but it's not yet something I experience as often as I'd like. It's a challenge for me to keep my gaze centered on His character—who He is and how He is—versus my tarnished perception. I have beautiful moments like I described above, but I also have those moments where my carnal nature rises and opens the door for questions, doubts, and accusations regarding God's character; in no time, my errant perception of Him will darken and ultimately snuff out the light I've been walking in, so it's important that I am deliberate in keeping Proverbs 3:11–12 close to my heart:

> My son, do not despise the Lord's discipline,
> and do not resent his rebuke,
> because the Lord disciplines those he loves,
> as a father the son he delights in.

A Father's Counsel & Guidance

Wisdom and understanding are qualities I learned to yearn for (from whoever was willing to give freely) because in many ways, I felt invisible as a child. I don't remember my mother ever really caring about what I thought or how I felt within our day-to-day interactions. In her home, it was always her way; there was no highway! So, I didn't really have much of a voice. My mom believed wholeheartedly in the boundaries between parent and child; she was no friend to me, and she made sure I understood that. Because of this dynamic, there was very little friendliness between us, and going to her for casual conversation was pretty rare. When I needed insight or clarity, going to my mom wasn't second nature for me. I don't recall too many times of feeling inclined to seek her out for advice and counsel. In fact, I don't recall having anyone I could go to. I'm pretty certain this was not the dynamic she desired or intended, and to be fair, I may have gone to her more than I remember through the years—I just don't remember more than a handful of moments in my life where I approached her, sat down with her, and received her wisdom and guidance. I don't doubt she was willing, but I don't remember her being very talkative. At least not with me, outside of very serious matters. And even then, it wasn't a two-way conversation; it was her addressing me while I remained primarily on the receiving end.

But she and I both remember how—after going long periods of time without having an outlet for my thoughts and emotions—I would get fed up inside and express myself through handwritten letters that I would give her. Looking back, I guess I've always been the type of person to have an opinion and perspective about everything around me, but never having an audience, feeling silenced, and believing that my feelings and perspective didn't matter to anyone cultivated in me an unnaturally quiet temperament. This I think caused me to swing to the other side of the spectrum in my adulthood, where I shouted from the mountaintop every feeling, thought, and opinion I had—and in some of the most direct ways possible. Add to this my insecurities, plus my ambitions, overachieving nature, and overcompensated self-worth, I became the typical aggressive and abrasive Type A personality. I've had to spend years learning how to gain balance so I could sit in the middle of my extremes. I've had to be purposeful in minding what God means when He admonishes us to have a gentle and quiet spirit (1 Pet 3:4). I've had to figure out what having the Fruit of the Spirit (Gal 5:22–23) actually looks, feels, and sounds like within my unique personality and balanced temperament.

Throughout my childhood and into my teen years, I didn't have anyone consistently imparting any substantial amount of knowledge or wisdom, not even my brother, who was five years older. He and I never had a relationship; things between us were always tense and distant, and I'm convinced he just never really liked me no matter what I did or didn't do. So, naturally, he had nothing to offer me. For instance, when I made an attempt to take my life, he was residing on the West coast, while serving in the military. I received a phone call from him and all I remember is his telling me (through what felt like sincere emotion) that there's never a reason to feel the need to take my life. I appreciated that phone call and encouragement, but he never followed up with me a day, a week, or even a month later to establish a connection with me or to even see how I was doing. That one phone call was all I received from him.

So, it has always been a desire of mine to have and be mentored, and I always had my eyes open for men and women who would take the time to listen and understand how I felt, what I thought, and how I formed my perspective—because I wanted them to be effective in providing correction and redirection. I observe very well and have a way with reading people and hearing deeper than what a person may actually be saying when conversing, but I have always been thirsty for a higher level of knowledge and understanding through impartation. I've always longed to be shaped and molded into my best self with the help of someone sincerely vested in me. I always want the best possible chance at being successful, both personally and professionally, and I'm still the same way for the most part. I have never been one to have issues with listening to people's advice and learning from others' mistakes. If it makes sense and will save me anything (time, energy, heartbreak, money, bad health, etc.), I'll implement it into my decision-making.

During one of my counseling sessions, I realized why this thirst played such a significant role in my gullibility and naïvety with the upperclassman who sexually assaulted me. I was so hungry for what I believed he was providing, when in reality he was just a predator who saw an empty pit just waiting to be exploited.

This area of my relationship with the Lord isn't as difficult as any of the others, but it definitely still needs to be redefined and reshaped.

> "If any of you lacks wisdom, you should ask God, who gives generously to all without finding fault, and it will be given to you." (Jas 1:5-6 NIV)

I need to start seeing God's wisdom and guidance through a different filter. Yes, He is God and He is my God, but I have to constantly remind myself that He is my Father and I am a priority to Him. My benefitting is paramount and carries the greatest importance to Him. This is a concept that's not advanced as often as I think it should be within the Christian circles I'm most familiar with. Way too many times over the years I've heard convincing arguments spoken declaring that virtually everything God does for me is primarily for the benefit of someone else: every adversity we personally endure is for the sole purpose of having a testimony that will impact someone else's life and circumstances; and somehow, I'm not the primary benefactor, essentially reduced to being something like a reservoir—a passageway for God's benefits, privileges, grace, and sufficiency to primarily flow through to others. What I hear from these teachings is that I am to settle for the moisture and scraps left behind, and I *should* be grateful and satisfied! I can't count the number of times I've heard this sentiment in both public and private circles, especially in instances where a believer is attempting to encourage another believer through their trial or storm. The intention may be good, but the principle isn't always fitting. I am absolutely a vessel, a collaborator, an ambassador, a messenger, and a servant. I believe my tests, trials, and tribulations are or will be used for the benefit of others. But in addition to this noble purpose, I believe I am first and foremost His child, and as such, I am the priority and primary benefactor of these circumstances. There is something in store for me to gain first, whether it be squeezing out virtue, pruning away unneeded/detrimental qualities, molding my temperament, or shaving my rough edges like sandpaper.

Not having the privilege of experiencing how amazing it is to have the wisdom and perspective of a man at my disposal is a tragedy. Every child deserves to have the wisdom and body of knowledge and experiences that can only come from a father or father figure. Men see the world differently, they internalize and process information differently, and they approach and handle situations differently than women do. They understand other men in ways that women will never truly be able to do, so their overall perspective on life is just as invaluable as a mother's. I can only imagine how having this blessing at my fingertips would have helped me navigate life a lot differently. I often hear fathered women express that who they have become is a direct result of their father's guidance through the years. I'm already convinced of how true this is, so it doesn't take much for me to savor God's wisdom and guidance (when I can get out of my flesh and carnal nature). It doesn't matter how or through whom He chooses to dispense or impart His heavenly truths and clarity—I'm completely open. Well, usually! It does take a little bit of effort sometimes to tune and then fine tune my ability to see, hear, and perceive what God is saying and how He may be leading me, but I have at least chosen to be intentional with seeing His wisdom and guidance through the lens of Him being more than just my God. He's leading, caring, and guiding me through His wisdom because He is *fathering* me. And I want to let Him father me.

A Father's Protection

A father's protection is by far the most challenging in my endeavor to allow the Holy Spirit to redefine and reshape fatherhood. Shifting my perception of Him and how I feel about Him in this area is beyond difficult because it's very complex and perplexing. The mental and emotional effort I've put forth so far is tedious and stressful even, because I've experienced what feels like God's complete lack of protection *and* vindication. I know full well the protection of a mother; she was my fierce protector and defender. She always had my back and singlehandedly made sure I knew I wasn't alone in the world, assuring me through her presence and example that I'll always have someone who will protect and advocate for me, whether I am dealing with a stranger, a teacher, a school bully, or a four-legged dog. She was definitely "about that life" if it came to it! Growing up, my mother didn't have this privilege; she never had anyone to protect and advocate for her, and at times her life and future felt incredibly bleak. She shared with me a few times that her greatest desire and earnest prayer was to simply live long enough to see my brother and me reach adulthood. I know what it feels like to be under the wing protection of a mom.

I also know what it feels like to be totally left exposed, unguarded, and vulnerable. I grapple with the belief that God failed me in this area on way too many occasions. The *One* person who has the power, ability, foresight, knowledge, and wisdom to protect me from all harm and defend me against all danger—both seen and unseen—failed to do what He's so capable of. As far as I'm concerned, two fathers have failed to protect and defend me.

Sometimes it is challenging for me to believe parts of the Bible like Psalm 121, which is one of David's testimonies regarding God's protection and how He's a keeper and will preserve us from evil and so on. In fact, it's more than just a challenge; it feels unreal and not applicable. I can appreciate David's testimony, and I'd love to believe that this level of protection, defense, and vindication is true and available to me as well, but within my heart, it's currently not a truth I can genuinely stand on yet within my heart.

What I do understand and have come to embrace and accept is this: life happens. I recognize and have accepted that we live in a fallen world where the will of mankind is not usurped in any way, shape, or form. Through the counseling sessions aimed at healing from the trauma of being sexually assaulted, I arrived at a place where I no longer placed fault at my own doorstep. I no longer blamed myself for the events that led up to the violation, and I also stopped blaming God for "allowing" it to happen the second time. And, although I've chosen not to lay blame on either of us anymore, that doesn't take away my inability to see the Lord as my protector and defender. I have a very long road ahead of me in this area, which is the primary reason why I can't sincerely declare, "Yes, I believe God has been good to me all of my life." It's just not something I believe yet. I understand there is still emotional healing to be had, and I fully expect it to arrive at some point soon. But until then, I can only continue being intentional with meditating on the following verse:

> So do not fear, for I am with you; do not be dismayed, for
> I am your God. I will strengthen you and help you; I will
> uphold you with my righteous right hand. (Isa 41:10)

I have every desire to get to the point where I can believe this for myself, but I have no intention of simply leaping over to this other side without having done the work. I'm not willing to simply declare anything about God with a heart full of doubt, and maybe even resentment and bitterness. I need to ensure my declaration of spiritual truths comes from the depth of my soul with authenticity and conviction. Again, the only exceptions are those times when I'm purposefully looking to shift myself internally and the atmosphere around me with an audible declaration of Scripture. I'm more than willing to speak life into myself and my circumstances, to call things what they are despite what they may look like. I've seen and experienced firsthand the power and change that comes when praying or declaring God's truth, using specific verses in the Bible. It's a beautiful and truly amazing thing to experience. But I always defer to speaking honestly, and as things move and shift within me (in my thoughts and emotions), they'll manifest outwardly (in my speech and behavior). This is my overall stance, but there is something brewing inside me that's echoing a sentiment I heard a few weeks ago.

I attended a simulcast with Priscilla Shirer and I remember her brother, who was leading praise and worship, mentioned that we shall declare the truth about God no matter how we feel. Imagine the pause I felt in my spirit when I heard that. It's a spiritual principle that I'm willing to get behind. I just have to get behind it.

Being in these trenches of learning to live loved isn't pretty by any stretch of the imagination, but I'll take walking hand-in-hand with the Holy Spirit through the ugliness wedged within my soul over living life as I had been any day.

Chapter 7

He Loves Me, He Loves Me Not

Does God love me?

But, of course He does. God *is* love!

And He loves me so much that He gave His only begotten son to die an undeserving death on a raggedy old rugged cross.

~

*N*ot only is this simply true, it's immeasurably profound and the very foundation upon which our faith and religion stand. Answering "Does God love me?" in the affirmative is by far the most automatic response a believer will offer when posed the question. Besides, how in the world could we dare say otherwise when the love of the God of the Bible may be one of the most familiar characteristics among unbelievers and the most adored characteristic among believers? Christians understand, even if only on a surface level, that God's love for us is the motive behind everything He does, has ever done, and will ever do.

But when I stop and reflect on the idea that God loves me, within a few deep pockets of my heart I have moments where my actual truth tells a different story. There are certain crevices within the folds of my heart that reflect a reality that I'm not necessarily embarrassed or ashamed of—because it's my truth—but there is a significant conflict within me. In many ways, this can be seen as the epitome of being an oxymoron. I'm able to manage an overall answer of "Yes, God loves me," but within these deeper folds, my belief in God's specific love for me isn't nearly as solid, steadfast, and immovable as it could be. In some instances, I'm still journeying from the posture that God simply loves me in the way that's available to all believers. My destination is to have the posture in my heart that confidently believes He loves me specifically and impartially.

My brokenness has always informed me of the idea that I get the short end of the stick far more often than not. Brokenness loves to believe that I'm not as exceptional or as extraordinary as I "should" be, at least not to the degree that would inspire God to freely love me just because I am me. This is where my overachieving nature thrived, which laid the foundation for my "works righteousness"[7] to flourish. I wasn't aware of my inclination to overachieve until my husband casually mentioned it during one of our conversations where we were reflecting on a previous argument. For as long as I can remember, I've always had the need to pursue and be excellent; I've always felt the need to prove myself, and not to anyone in particular. Sometimes the personal satisfaction was enough, except in relationships. I always believed it was easy to overlook qualities in me that I believed were endearing and worth being recognized, so I put forth the effort to make sure they were noticed. In many ways, this works out because I have very high standards and work really hard to meet them; nonetheless, being balanced is important to me. I'm now capable of being a high achiever in any endeavor I put onto my plate, and the results of my work usually show excellence. But when I'm imbalanced, it not only affects my work and my output, it also causes undue stress which can seep into my relationships. My expectations of people can be too high, bringing about feelings of failure, disappointment, etc. Only in my thirties did I begin to sit comfortably in who I am natively, resting in who I am naturally. My husband, being on the other end of the

---

7 Works righteousness is about earning God's love, blessings, one's way to heaven, etc., which is in contrast to righteousness through faith in Jesus Christ alone.

spectrum, has helped me tremendously in balancing this out. I no longer have the need to prove myself or go significantly beyond the call or task. But works righteousness still has a way of creeping in and magnetically pulling in those thoughts that I'm not good enough. Even in my thirties, it's interesting how these doubts can cross my mind: my earthly father didn't love me enough to be in my life, so why and how can I expect a Heavenly Father to be any different, especially when there are bazillions of humans to compete with?

I can easily suppress these and the many other thoughts and feelings that are in constant conflict with everything I know and desire to believe; this helps me exist neatly within the boundaries of Christian thought and beliefs, but I'm just not built for that kind of in such a way that allows me to live in that self-deception. When my mind is quiet enough, when I'm still enough to allow the truth of those folds within my heart to emerge—especially during trying events and circumstances—I can clearly see how years of living as a mere subject attempting to serve at the Lord's pleasure has nurtured so many doubts about His love for me. Despite the progress I've made over the years, and continue to make, I still have moments where I believe I am purposed to receive the crumbs that fall from His table—and how dare I have anything less than gratefulness in my heart for these crumbs?! Other times, I see the giant I am in Christ. Or, I see the beast I've been when it comes to spiritual things. Similar to the Prophet Elijah in 1 Kings 18, who had unmistakable boldness in God and immeasurable amounts of faith when contending with and defeating the prophets of Baal, but in chapter 19, we see a totally different prophet. He didn't respond to his adversaries in the way I would expect him to, considering what he had just done in the name of the Lord. Sometimes, my insecurity takes me to a place where I can only trust God as far as I can "see" Him, which brings about a snowball effect, because then I feel some level of guilt because my reality is that sometimes I just don't trust the Lord.

I recognize how taboo it is to not only feel these things but to actually say them aloud. It's almost an abomination in some Christian circles to admit even half of the challenges I have as a believer who may be called to be a leader—especially after having had opportunities to stand behind the pulpit, Bible in hand, proclaiming "Thus says the Lord." When we are leaders in any capacity, if we've shown ourselves to have a calling on our lives, especially within the five-fold ministry (i.e., apostle, prophet, evangelist, pastor, and teacher), it's as if we are forbidden from having any significant doubts about the faith, let alone God. At least not publicly!

However, I do have the privilege of being privy to and have many examples of believers who genuinely live full and vibrant lives in Christ, as much as they know how. They seem to be the recipients of unlimited revelation from the Holy Spirit; they see miracles, signs, and wonders, and they walk in joy and abundance every day of their lives because of their uncanny ability to take hold of Scripture and operate within its full power. That's not to say they don't have doubts, struggles, or insecurities; they simply have an uncanny ability to overcome those internal challenges, and I appreciate their transparency during those seasons or moments when they choose to share. I consider them my Christian elite, and I enjoy living vicariously through these believers. Sometimes, I wonder what it is about them or what they have done that allows them to have been selected among those few who float in the so-called unfair, special, and rare favor of the Lord.

On the other hand, I see way too many examples of believers in various circles who are constantly struggling from day to day in their walk and relationship with the Lord, constantly unhappy and griping while trying to find and keep the joy of the Lord. It takes nothing for me to feel helpless and sometimes hopeless in instances where they are continually missing countless opportunities and being passed over on some of the simplest of things. But, I am compelled to continue walking hand-in-hand with those who find themselves struggling or even stagnant within their walk with the Lord, at least in those areas where I've matured and can do so.

But I've become tired of living vicariously through fellow peers who seem to have it all in Christ. I've grown tired of picking daisy petals off one by one in order to gain an inkling of how much God's love surrounds me this day, this week, or this season of my life. I no longer want to be a type of prodigal daughter who can live the good life in the Father's house in one season and in the next season believe I deserve and will receive not much more than what a servant is entitled to. I'm tired of the narrative of fatherlessness when all I need to do is learn how to exist and live in the unconditional love of the men God has specifically handpicked for me. I've had to start refocusing my attention and shifting my gaze onto my right-now season so that I can see, appreciate, and begin living an even fuller life in the present.

Godsent Civil Engineer

When I walked into the arms of salvation on my living room floor, the woman on the other end of the phone discipled and mentored me those first few years as a believer in a very loving, intentional, and consistent way. We adopted each other as godmother and goddaughter, and she laid the foundation for my life as a believer—how to pray, how to hear God's voice, praying in the heavenly language, reading the Bible regularly, the need to memorize Scripture verses, how to grow my faith and use it effectively, how to live holy and strip away behaviors that were un-Christlike, etc. All of this meant everything to me, but I was starting to become desperate to join a church. Especially being a textbook extrovert, I was in desperate need of contact with other believers. I wanted to gain a church family and develop relationships with other believers who were on the same path as me. I was ready to learn and grow in different ways—alongside some folks I could touch.

When I relocated to the Washington, DC, area, I regularly visited different churches, but I could not for the life of me find one that felt right, and the disappointment was mounting. Finally, one morning on the metro I heard a woman across the aisle from me listening to a song by Fred Hammond through her headphones. As we were getting off the train, I tapped her on her shoulder and asked what church she attended; she told me about a church called Greater Mount Calvary Holy Church in Northeast that I'd be able to see right from the metro platform. The very next Sunday, I took the train to that church and finally found my church home, despite it being a mega church! I didn't know any better though. When I arrived, it was like being on a college campus, and that was right up my alley.

I had no problem acclimating. It took me no time to become heavily involved and plugged into many of the ministries available—Women's Ministry, Young Adult Ministry, Singles' Ministry, Liturgical Dance Ministry, Mime Ministry, and I even did a stint as a member of one of the choirs (which is notable because although I can carry a note pretty decently, I sound like Mary J. Blige before voice lessons, and as far as I'm concerned, that's actually kind of dope!). I attended a few different Bible studies throughout the week, and I adored my leaders Bishop Alfred A. Owens and Co-Pastor Susie C. Owens. I began falling in love with the Lord and grew exponentially in Him and in life in general. I had a number of hard, cold, and dry seasons while living on my own and living life in DC, but I think I managed pretty well (at least externally) despite those trials and storms.

One Sunday, after hearing an announcement about a more formalized biblical education I could receive through the church's ministry called the Calvary Bible Institute, I decided to attend one of their informational sessions to learn more about the institute and their certificate programs. I was totally sold! At the time, I was at the beginning of rebuilding from being unemployed for almost a year, so I didn't anticipate being able to pursue any of their certificate programs immediately. But I wanted to prepare for it because my mind was made up; I would be moving forward with a more formalized education.

After the session, I walked up to the gentleman behind the table handling the brochures, catalog, and other paperwork, and I inquired about the cost of the courses. We had a casual back and forth, but I eventually realized, for whatever reason, he would not answer my question! He kept asking me which certificate program I was interested in and which courses I was most interested in, and although I didn't mind sharing, I was more concerned about the cost. I asked again about the cost, and he answered by asking what semester I was interested in starting my studies. At this point, to say I was getting frustrated is an understatement. I couldn't understand for the life of me why this man, who didn't know me from a can of paint, was refusing to answer such a basic question—a question I imagine any normal person would be interested in knowing. I was ready to rock and roll and see what my chances were of being able to actually pursue studying there. I tried explaining to him that I was coming off of being unemployed for an extended amount of time and needed to know the cost of the courses so I could know what to save once things changed for me. That man never answered my question! He instructed me to come see him in his office during the week, and all I could do was walk away from that table with the course catalog in my hand and a boatload of sarcasm in my eyebrows. I was being tormented by the descriptions of all these wonderful courses that piqued my interest, while having no clue as to whether I'd be able to enjoy attending any of them. Looking back, I don't understand why the prices weren't in the catalog to begin with!

But trust and believe I did, as the man told me to. That same week, I got on the metro and went to his office up the street from the church where the institute held its administrative offices. I came to know the man as Minister Thornton, the registrar for the institute. When I arrived at his office, he seemed pleasantly surprised and invited me to sit down at his desk across from him. He and I chatted about normal stuff about life, where I was from, how I ended up in DC, what I did for a living, etc. It was a very pleasant conversation, and before I knew it, I was totally lost in his genuine interest in me. When we finally got around to talking about the courses, we landed on the two I would likely begin with, and he informed me I would start when classes began that upcoming semester (which was a few weeks away). I immediately protested because I knew I didn't have the money, no matter what the courses cost! But he cut me off midprotest, letting me know he would be paying for the courses. When I heard that, the room fell silent.

At the time, I had no idea that the bridge my biological father had collapsed and left in ruins for over two decades was being reconstructed. God caused me to cross paths with a man who would rebuild my pathway to Him. Minister Thornton was given (and accepted with immense joy) a divine assignment, giving an abandoned and fatherless young woman the opportunity to experience the many privileges and benefits she missed out on her entire life. Using God's blueprint, Minister Thornton began reconstructing the bridge that would allow me to begin finding my way to the Lord, giving me the chance to understand and see Him for the Father He is.

In the beginning, I would visit Minister Thornton after work a few days a week to offer my administrative skills. I never felt indebted to him, but I wanted to offer something as an expression of my thankfulness for his generosity toward me and my appreciation for there being no strings attached. Interestingly enough, I never really did much except sit with him and talk. I didn't realize it at the time, but he was getting to know me; he was learning and understanding me and the many areas of my brokenness. I had become so comfortable with him that it never dawned on me what the actual purpose and intent of our interaction would be. I just lived in his presence and all that he effortlessly poured into me, while expecting absolutely nothing in return. I began to spend time with him and his wife Angela, hanging out at their home in Southeast, DC, and they immersed me in DC life and the beauty (sometimes rugged beauty) of the city and surrounding suburbs. I don't remember when, and I can't remember the surrounding circumstances, but our relationship had become such that I asked Minister Thornton if I could call him Pops. I wasn't sure how to call anyone *Dad*; I was an adult and Pops just felt like an alternative that honored him and the significance of who he had become in my life.

Through my relationship with him, I continued to experience many, if not all, of the wonders of what it is to be fathered. I can absolutely feel his love for me, and it is truly unconditional. He enjoyed being around me just as much as I enjoyed being around him. We would take walks around his community, roll up our pant legs, stick our feet in the community pool, and chat. He would call me often to check on me and other times just to hear my voice. I would ask his opinion on various things, and he always shared his opinion and perspective from the standpoint of a father guiding his daughter on the ways of the world, life, and love. He was the first man to give me a teddy bear. I'm pretty sure I asked for it, though. I think I wanted something I never had before, and sure enough, he got me one from Build-a-Bear, complete with the voice recording and everything! He was the first man to send me flowers to my job and taught me "whenever you're with me, your hand shall never touch a doorknob." He became my standard for what qualities I desired in a husband, and I understood what it felt like to be treated so well.

My husband Ivan, was just a friend at the time. We actually met online through a website called Blackplanet.com, and although he was not shy about his interest in me, I had no desire to be in a long-distance relationship. My heart was set on being married and being found by the man that God had specifically set aside for me. Since Ivan was living in New Orleans, it was obvious he wasn't the man God had in mind! Over the course of some months, he and I developed a beautiful friendship, one I had never experienced before. Our communication transitioned through the first few months. First, it was through inbox messages, then I upgraded him to instant messaging, and then finally I upgraded us to talking on the phone. The song wasn't out then, but you can imagine how much I enjoy Beyoncé's song, "Upgrade U!" Knowing Ivan's interest in having a relationship never deterred me from the principle that a longdistance relationship wasn't ideal for me at that point, and I figured he wasn't too serious about being with me on any level that was meaningful because he wasn't willing to consider relocating closer to the DC area.

Hurricane Katrina made her way to the States, and Ivan, living in the ninth ward, where the levees broke, landed him in the position of being homeless, shuffling around until hotel accommodations from FEMA kicked in. Communication was difficult because of cell phone towers being down, but he kept me in the loop as much as he could. During one of our conversations, I offered to house him temporarily in my efficiency apartment until he was able to find employment and get on his feet (I'm going to completely gloss over the idiocy of such an offer and arrangement!), and I kept this from my Pops. Somehow, he found out anyway. He came by my apartment and whisked Ivan away without saying a word to me. Later that day, they came back and Ivan had signed a new lease for an apartment about three blocks from mine that he would be able to move into immediately! This action by my Pops set the course for me and Ivan to enter into marriage without having crossed the line of sexual sin, which would have come much easier in the cohabitating arrangement that had been previously (and innocently) set up. He wisely protected and preserved me—and the sanctity of our marriage. He ensured I received the gift we knew I wanted so badly but would have likely ruined.

I also can't remember when I asked if I could call him Dad, but it was certainly fitting as far as I was concerned. And again, he obliged. He gave me the gift of having and experiencing what it's like to have a dad. It doesn't matter that I was already in my twenties when the experience of being fathered finally arrived. And he finally finished rebuilding the bridge that would safely land me on the other side, and it's extremely heartwarming to be able to say, "I'm finally here." I finally have the ability to begin navigating toward my Heavenly Father, and I'm traversing this new land with the wisdom and guidance of a father figure who knows the lay of the land very well.

Having this loving dad has significantly reduced the number of times I find myself picking the petals off a daisy in my quest to figure out if God loves me; he lessened how often I find myself wrestling with God's love for me during those difficult seasons where the question itself has the gall to emerge. Sometimes, my soul just wants to remain bent toward believing—when things are going well—I'm doing what God expects and desires, and He is therefore loving me in return and allowing blessings. And when things aren't going well, or when the storms of life rage, it could be an indication that He's not pleased with me and may be allowing the storm, or could be withholding His protection, blessings, etc. I have to take responsibility for this, though. I have to choose to remember that I have a relentless and formidable enemy who wants nothing more than for me to accuse God, doubt Him, and spiral toward spiritual apathy until I find myself sinking in the sludge of hopelessness, anxiety, and depression. Instead, I have to continually choose to recall and find strength in the numerous seasons and situations where I trusted God with the heart of a child and believed there was nothing He wouldn't do for me—and actually experienced Him move Heaven and earth to get through to little ol' me!

Chapter 8

Triune Beingness

For a long time, I had a firm grip on how I was doing life, and I kept a death grip on the things I created around me that provided me with my *idea* of safety, security, and control. But the need for a paradigm shift came tumbling down my street and landed on my front porch. My understanding of a paradigm shift is a fundamental change in a person's view of how people and things work. So, to release either of my grips in any way, especially my death grip, felt like the equivalent of being uncovered and exposed. The shelter of various walls I meticulously constructed for myself and reinforced through the years was now on the cusp of being bulldozed and demolished, revealing all my vulnerabilities, insecurities, and other points of weakness. Probably one of the most heart-wrenching feelings I've struggled with is being required to relinquish all control *I believed* I had over my life (and the people I held closest to my heart). Control had become somewhat of an idol; it was what I used to protect myself from any form of danger or opposition I perceived coming my way. But eventually the sacrifices I needed to make in order to reach my greater goal and realize the vision I had for myself became significantly more important than holding on to my fears, preserving those erected walls and protecting my learned inclinations and behaviors. I decided to trade in the familiar for the unfamiliar so the shift toward living life on the opposite side of brokenness, emotional instability, and dysfunction could be realized— and extend way beyond the surface of religion or religious rhetoric and practices.

Doing the mental and emotional work of pivoting away from what had become my norm was beyond exhausting. The process of shifting and being transformed is something you have to work at with every ounce of consistent diligence and might you can muster. And the only way to move forward is to simply move forward.

When I received my first significant, and most transformative breakthrough during my sessions in Christian counseling, I dared not to end my counseling in celebration of such a life-changing milestone. It was indeed something worth celebrating, but that specific moment in my life mirrored something similar to the birth of a child. I was brand new in my perspective and the way I would view and interact with the world and the people I encountered, from strangers on the sidewalk to my husband; everything was now new and unfamiliar. And, although I had a mental and emotional breakthrough that added to and intensified my spiritual overhaul, my paradigm and the way I functioned internally still needed to continue shifting . . . and quite dramatically. So, it was crucial for me to continue my counseling sessions. I still needed to be guided within the newness I was experiencing. On one hand, I felt like this newness was an abrupt change, even though the process was slow and gradual. I still had many things to continue unlearning and reversing while simultaneously learning how to function and operate within my new understanding and mindset regarding the world around me. Being liberated to this degree carried with it a drastically different set of systems and boundaries, and I needed to hold my counselor's hand for just a little while longer to ensure I didn't regress into any of my unhealthy and dysfunctional ways of thinking, believing, reacting, and responding. I was unbelievably fragile, and as I grew and developed at what felt like the speed of light, it was imperative that I gained the tools that would allow me to stay the course with as minimal distractions and diversions as possible. Being able to walk and function completely on my own within this new dynamic was all that mattered. Dependency on my counselor or the counseling sessions wasn't a desire, need, or intention (although the comfort and safety of these sessions was a bummer to let go of when the time finally rolled around), but thankfully, I received and acted on the wisdom to continue with a few more sessions during the most delicate and feeble part of my transition.

The Revelation

During these sessions where I felt like I was in something like a spiritual incubator, there were other resources pouring into me, helping me along my new path. I came across a teaching on YouTube called "How to Win Your Faith Fight," by Pastors Tyrone and Cynthia Marshall of Victory Christian Ministries International in Northeast, DC. As far as I can remember, I've always had a need to understand or at least be able to identify the *why* behind everything. I am a true get-to-the-root-of-everything kind of person, and being this way has always driven how I receive and interpret information, view people, view circumstances surrounding me, and translate the behaviors and actions of others. For me, there is a *why* beneath every feeling and emotion, which is what ultimately informs all reactions and behaviors. This teaching helped reshape my understanding of how I operate both when I'm at my highest point and when I'm at my lowest. The most meaningful part of that teaching for me was when Pastor Cynthia expounds on how we are constantly living beneath our God-given privilege as believers because we don't truly understand our triune nature, who we really are, and how we are meant to function within the earthly realm.

I've placed the Scripture references she used within her teaching at the end of this chapter, but in a nutshell, Pastor Cynthia explained how we are made up of three parts: body (flesh), soul, and spirit—and our *real* identity resides within and only within our spirit (or what many like to refer to as our spirit man). She talks about how we are dangerously in tune with and governed by our soul, which is the place where we think, choose, and feel through our mind, will, and emotions. For example, she cites that often we are consumed with thoughts and feelings concerning things like our vocations, how to compete and advance in our careers, bills and finances, marital issues or difficulties in romantic relationships, parenting and co-parenting challenges, etc. We have a tendency to obsess about how we see and feel about our circumstances, and we are usually capable of understanding and expressing our thoughts and feelings in a number of different ways—and through various platforms—because we are so in tune with these aspects of our lives via our soul.

After being governed by our soul, we then mistakenly prioritize our flesh. She talks about how we spend a great deal of time focusing on our bodies and the maintenance of ourselves, constantly discovering and understanding how we experience the world around us through our five senses, all the while completely neglecting the third part of our nature, which is our spirit. We don't usually know much of anything about our spirit or how in the world it happens to be the place where our true identity dwells. We don't usually know how our spirit operates, what our spirit needs, or how it impacts our dayto-day lives. We can be absolutely clueless about the role our spirit plays within our experience of life and how we interact with our world.

At this point within her teaching, Pastor Cynthia demonstrated how 1) our spirit carries our true identity, which 2) influences our soul, and 3) lives in a body. She uses Adam in the Garden of Eden as an example: life did not begin for him until God breathed the breath of life through his nostrils. Through her demonstration, what she was teaching began to make perfect sense as I recognized the fact that my flesh isn't who I am; it is the mere vehicle I use to transport who I really am (my spirit), and it is nothing more than the vehicle that allows me to interact and communicate within the natural world (using my five senses). So, because my spirit is something I can't necessarily perceive, feel, or sense like I can everything else, it's essentially out of sight and out of mind.

The overarching revelation for me is 1) the understanding that my soul is the bridge between the physical (visible) world and the spiritual (invisible) realm and 2) that I am supposed to be navigating between the two, transferring things from the invisible realm over into the physical world. My soul, (which is where all my thoughts, feelings, and decision-making dwell) was designed to be completely influenced and shaped by my spirit. This influence is then reflected in my body through what I declare and how I behave.

To be practical, I have two basic options: spend time praying, worshiping, reading and meditating on Scripture—*or* don't. On the one hand, I can feed myself spiritually what is necessary to fuel my soul with everything it needs to feel, think, and choose according to what lines up with the Lord, which will all manifest through my physical body. Or I can neglect to feed my spirit spiritual things, which consequently starves my soul and causes me to operate in the natural and physical world outside of biblical and spiritual truths.

This demonstration really resonated with me because I can relate to the results of both. Just recently (within the last few months), I had been operating from the position of neglecting to feed my spirit spiritual things. I hadn't been spending *any* meaningful time in the Word or anything close to quality time in prayer. Personal worship had been a dismal experience, considering what I'm used to, and I had also been neglecting to consistently assemble and fellowship with other believers within the four walls of my local church. One afternoon, I had a sobering conversation with a good friend and sister, Rochelle. She saw a comment I made on Facebook, and she left me a message expressing her loving disgust for what she recognized as my complete lack of faith and defeatist mentality. She knows me, and she knows me well. She has experienced firsthand what I'm capable of when I'm fully walking in the grace, sufficiency, and power of God.

When she called me to the carpet, she gave me the space to share my heart, which helped me to recognize for myself my spiritual condition at that point. I had been existing in a state where I was easily and constantly overwhelmed emotionally, mentally defeated, lacking in faith, and completely deficient in both spiritual and natural foresight, making life way more difficult for myself than it had to be. Starving myself spiritually was like a domino effect that ultimately manifested in my body several different ways. Throughout the preceding weeks, I had a very short fuse when it came to my daily interactions with my toddlers. Frustration and irritation were through the roof moment by moment, and it took everything in me not to be unreasonable, impatient, and mean toward them. All of which I failed miserably, many days. I had moments where I wanted to have a meltdown because I felt overwhelmed with simple things, like failing to meal plan, which led to my family not eating as properly as I intended. So then guilt built as I struggled to pull it together. I had to work to keep headaches at bay, and in the instances when that failed, I had to pull out my tension headache medicine, which also bothered me, but that's a different book! I didn't have the desire or energy to do things excellently when it came to my entrepreneurial endeavors or my non-profit organizations. I promise I can keep listing all the ways I was a complete ball of mess. I was managing as well as I could within my humanity and carnal nature, but the winds and waves of normal life were tossing me around like a tugboat in the middle of a sea whose captain decided to stop being the captain. I ultimately just needed to get my life!

The very next day, I did exactly that. Although Rochelle found me existing in a state where I was being ruled and governed by my fears, allowing unhealthy and unfruitful thoughts and feelings to take root which influenced my behavior, my first course of action was to make a plan I would execute immediately. The moment I opened my eyes the first thing I did was talk to God and handed over to Him everything I had been carrying. I rolled out of bed, and on my way to greet my toddlers and get the day started, I decided to go back to the basics: 2 Corinthians 10:5, which directs us to take every thought captive into the obedience of Christ (which I talk about this in the next chapter.) Everything for me starts with this verse. I started monitoring my thoughts and redirecting them appropriately. So, when I began thinking of failure, I redirected that thought by telling myself *God has given me power to gain wealth* or that *I can do all things through Christ who is strengthening me in this very moment.* When I began to feel fear regarding the health of either of my sons, I resorted to the fact that God has not given me the spirit of fear, He has given me love, power, and a sound mind. I made a few phone calls to my partners and colleagues and tapped myself back into the ring. I decided I would accompany Rochelle to a women's event at one of our churches in the community that following Sunday. I committed to attending the morning worship service prior to the woman's event, and I turned on YouTube and listened to a sermon from Priscilla Shirer that spoke to my heart to the point of tears. Effectively, getting my life!

Understanding that my spirit is who I am—that it is regenerated and needs to be constantly nourished with the things that are truly life-giving— really helps in pushing me toward being the type of woman in God I desire to be. One of the things which I can emphatically declare has been the primary reason for my overall growth as a believer is my habit of reading the Bible on a regular basis. Being proactive with changing the course of my life—and deciding to pivot away from what has been such a normal way of thinking, feeling, and choosing—has been successful by far simply due to consistently reading (and listening to) the Scriptures. This has always been my launching pad and the foundation through which I cultivated my prayer life and personal worship experience. Reading the Bible will literally make you pause, close your eyes, and ask God, "What in the world are you doing . . . ?" or "OK, God, now explain this to me, because I'm upset with how you handled this . . . ." That's prayer!! After reading a certain passage, I may be moved to turn on a song from Donnie Mclurkin, Mali Music, or Switch. Reading a different series of verses and now I want to rock out to Bizzle, Lecrae, KB, Trip Lee, or Andy Mineo! I've just moved into a space of personal praise and worship!

Now, I'm not at all minimizing Sunday morning worship service, nor am I diminishing the preached Word, but preaching and formal teaching within the four walls of a physical building are things I have never placed above simply reading the Bible for myself and privately experiencing God in a genuine way. This may certainly be the case because of how I was discipled by my very hands-on mentor and godmother. Because my journey as a believer began outside the four walls of a physical church, and because I remained there during my most formative years, the extremely high value many Christians place on the preached Word (and the Sunday morning worship experience) is not something I share or can relate to.

Don't get me wrong, preaching and teaching over the sacred desk is vital within the life of a believer. Assembling together and fellowshipping with other believers on a regular basis is absolutely necessary within the lives of all believers. In fact, we're instructed in the Bible not to forsake these things. I've just never subscribed to relying on this one dimension of the Christian life being most important or having the most impact on my overall Christian experience—and it never served as the bulk of how I live my life in Christ. To take my point further, reading the Bible regularly was reinforced once I finally found and became a member of Greater Mount Calvary Holy Church! I remember, during one of my first couple of worship services, I sat near the front of the stage while my co-pastor was preaching. At one point during her introduction, she said, "Ya'll know the story of Joseph . . . ," and I remember thinking to myself, *Uuuh, no. I don't actually.* I had no idea who Joseph was; I spent most of my time reading the New Testament. But that was the moment I decided to take reading the Bible to the next level and read it from cover to cover; although I was able to follow her message well, I knew my understanding and worship experience could be so much richer. And I fell in love with the Old Testament!

So of course, I have become a serious advocate for Christians actually sitting down and spending time reading the *one* sacred book that is the absolute center and foundation of our faith. I don't believe the expectation is that we all become biblical scholars in the sense that we all have and carry degrees and credentials, but I do think we should be studious, constantly growing in our knowledge and understanding of what God has inspired, revealed, and preserved specifically for us. I do think it's our individual responsibility—if we name the name of Christ as our Lord and consider ourselves believers—to read our sacred text so we can live out our lives in Christ the way He always intended (see 2 Timothy 2:15 and 3:16).

So, this is what I do. But beyond setting aside time to read the Bible like it's the greatest book known to mankind (I just realized the irony there!), I'm now learning how to personalize certain verses specifically aimed at building myself up within the view of my Father-daughter relationship with the Lord. I still have many seasons of drought and times where I am nowhere as disciplined as I can or should be. As I shared, I *just* came out of a drought! I'm not at all above being the first to admit that I can be one of the most consistently inconsistent people when it comes to reading and praying regularly when life chooses to take a few swings at me. I can be on fire for seven consecutive months and then fall out of the heavens at the drop of a dime and go weeks without opening my Bible. I can easily take the lazy route and play some Gospel and Christian music through Google Play or Pandora for background noise when I know my spirit is aching for that intimate time of pure worship—where I sit on the edge of my bed singing to Him a song I love— a cappella from the depth of my soul. I hate these dry and parched seasons but I've become a lot easier on myself having accepted the reality that current life circumstances, being a mother to toddlers, do not afford these same kinds of moments as often as I would like. In no way can these become excuses for entering spaces of spiritual malnourishment or reasons for remaining there for prolonged periods of time. Yes, God understands and knows my heart, but I still have the responsibility of when I recognize the state of my spirit, I need to do the work of climbing out of these dry patches so I can stop my soul and my body from regressing. Plus, I would much rather get back on track on my own rather than have a circumstance get my attention and hurl me back onto my game. I hate when life and the circumstances around me influence my soul rather than my spirit, filled with spiritual truths. I can more easily recognize when my soul is gazing at a spirit that is deadening, and more than that, it's a great feeling to know what all it takes to work with the Holy Spirit as I allow Him to breathe life back into me.

Scripture References from Pastors Tyrone and Cynthia Marshall's teaching:

1 Thessalonians 5:23; John 4:24; John 6:63; Genesis 2:7; James 2:26; 2 Corinthians 3:18; James 1

Chapter 9

Conquering My Thought Life

Beginning this chapter felt rather daunting because one of my most formidable battles has always been in my mind. Taking control of my thought life has been a war I feel I've won overall through the concept and exercise of the second part of 2 Corinthians 10:5:

"...take every thought captive into the obedience of Christ."

But the war will probably always rage. I win significantly more than I lose, but the back-and-forth I experience has become a part of my spiritual life. I've accepted this (at least for now) as part of my new norm. As I progress in my relationship with the Lord, the landscape where spiritual warfare begins looks a bit different and the strategies Satan and demonic influences employ against me seem to be constantly evolving at the same rate I grow and evolve. Fortunately, my weapons for fighting back have not needed to evolve or change, but my fight can sometimes be an everyday battle. Taking my thoughts captive can be a consecutive moment-by-moment brawl because, plain and simple, the enemy has no chill.

I often experience just how adamant Satan is. He is very aggressive in his objective to keep me bound within my soul in any way he can, he is extremely resolute in his aim to keep me confined for as long as possible within any form of mental prison strategically designed and fashioned to use *me*, to destroy me. Because my nature is naturally inclined to satisfy itself in ways that typically oppose God, when my spirit is malnourished, it's an easy job for Satan as I'll naturally work in unison with his tactics. I know what it feels like both pre- and post- salvation to be used as a tool in my own demise.

Sometimes my battle begins with a subtle distraction from doing something the Holy Spirit has instructed me to do. It can be as simple as increasing my time reading the Bible by five or ten minutes. Or waking up an hour early to start a morning routine with Him before my toddlers awaken for the day. Or He'll instruct me to be consistent in attending Sunday morning worship service for two months. Satan is very effective in his ability to tap into certain areas that seem inconsequential in the grand scheme of things, when in reality these things can have a significant impact on my overall spiritual health, well-being, and progress. Instead of extending my time reading the Bible, I may put it down altogether for a few days because I've finished a book and figure I'll just take a break. Those few days turn into a few weeks. Instead of waking up an hour early because I'm no longer a morning person, I decide to extend my evening by an hour to compensate. But that never happens because I realize, oh, I need to give my husband and our marriage some quality time, and it can only happen once the kids are down for the night. I've made the commitment to attend worship service on Sunday mornings, but by week three, I'd be too tired from date night with my husband. I sleep in and miss my window for getting ready, and it's no biggie—but missing one week then turns into four weeks. Being distracted in these areas easily diverts me clean off my path, causing me to have the potential of wandering in a direction I have no business traveling, especially since I have no idea what may be lying ahead of me that the Holy Spirit may be trying to prepare me for.

I can't for the life of me remember my age, so guessing is extremely difficult, but I'll guesstimate that I was probably around eight or nine years old. I remember I used to wake up on the weekends and lay in my bed for no less than two hours with my eyes wide open, daydreaming. I created actual soap operas in my mind, complete with characters, names, scenes, and scenarios that evolved as I evolved. When I was exposed to more complex life events and interesting scenarios from day-to-day, I would bring those situations into the lives of my characters, and those soap operas always ended on a to-be-continued basis. And, like clockwork, they would pick up right where I left off. I want to believe I was influenced by my mother's affinity for an actual soap opera she used to enjoy watching on TV called *The Young and the Restless*, but I hated that program and never spent any amount of time watching it on the days I happened to be home from school. So, I'm not sure what influenced me to do this, if there was anything at all. What I do know is that this habit I developed exercised the mental muscle that gives me the ability to tap out of reality whenever I choose, daydreaming and imagining an alternative life in very vivid, elaborate, and complex ways.

At some point along this path, I developed the capacity for some of the most dysfunctional and destructive thoughts to provide me with a sense of comfort and security. For instance, I cultivated this idea that in order to feel loved by a man I was in a romantic relationship with, he would need to cheat on me. So, I would create a scenario that involved me as the main character being in this romantic relationship and eventually finding out about him cheating. My male character would become obsessed with trying to convince me of just how much he loved me and regretted what he had done.

As I sit here typing this, I have absolutely no idea what type of dysfunctional relationship(s) I could have been privy to, in reality or on TV, that would influence me to think along these lines and mentally live in that kind of world. Grasping at straws here, I wonder if I somehow internalized the desire for my biological father to fight for and pursue me despite his mistake to abandon me. There is something within the pursuit of a man after he has made a huge mistake that equated to the only way I can feel his love. I've had *years* of practice perfecting these types of dysfunctional and unhealthy thought patterns that must have seeped into my actual reality. In this moment, I'm not able to dig through the layers, unearth, and begin assessing and analyzing this phenomenon within me, but for the longest time, normal things like quality time, loving and affirming words, and gifts never mentally conveyed love or affection for me, although I can absolutely feel love when I receive or experience these things. It's a blessing that this hasn't affected my marriage, but perhaps that's a product of something I have yet to discover. But, getting back to my point, I've had a significant number of years and loads of practice allowing my human, unregenerate, and carnal nature (and demonic influences) to have an authority over my soul that only the power of the Holy Spirit and His written Word has the ability to break and maintain.

Although I don't believe I'm the only one who battled with these types of thoughts, so far not too many people have expressed their ability to relate. I've received a lot of understanding and even a few raised eyebrows, but not too many "You know what? Me too" types of responses when I choose to share the struggles I've had on the battlefield of the mind. Perhaps I am rare in this area, but I wonder if I've just overcome the discomfort, shame, and embarrassment of it all, which enables me to speak freely about it in ways that others aren't yet comfortable with. Perhaps this level of exposure of internal thoughts and vulnerability is way too much for folks who may actually be able to relate privately. One thing I do know is we are all bombarded with various thoughts every second of each day because that's just the reality of the brain and how it works.

When the time came to begin putting in the work to pivot from where I was to where I wanted to be, the first choice I had to make was to take my belief in the power and authority of the Bible to a new level. I had to choose to believe what the Bible says and begin audibly declaring the various Scriptures that applied to whatever I was grappling with. How critical this is feels so indescribable, despite having an entire keyboard at my fingertips! To make this process practical and doable, I decided that whenever I came across various Scriptures when reading or listening to something, I'd write them down on colored index cards. In the beginning of my life as a believer, I was never one to memorize Scripture because I simply read the Bible like a novel. But when the temptation to daydream, or when unhealthy or crazy thoughts crossed my mind, I didn't have any specific Scriptures to counter those thoughts. This exercise was a game changer for me. Over time, I had a collection of index cards with a gazillion different Scriptures on them that I flipped through like a rolodex. Sometimes one verse served as my Scripture for the week, and I read it multiple times a day. After a while, I began stacking and had weekly and daily verses; then I added morning, afternoon, and evening verses. I believe this is a type of meditating on the Word day and night that the Bible instructs us to do in Joshua 1:8, but this also fueled my memorization of Scripture. I became proficient in declaring whatever verse(s) opposed and resisted anything I found myself thinking or feeling that was in conflict with Scripture.

But the beginning of my plight to monitor my *every* thought and take *every* thought into captivity using my index cards was obnoxiously overwhelming. There is no way for me to exaggerate my first week if I tried. Those first couple of days, I was bombarded by a machine gun of thoughts that covered the entire spectrum of life—from important day-to-day life situations to sheer foolishness. And this machine gun loaded with thoughts never ran out of ammunition. Beyond being over-whelmed, I oftentimes felt like I had started an impossible undertaking. In the same breath, it was a testament to the fact that a mind left unchecked and permitted to wander without boundaries can turn a life upside down. I literally had to sit still and read 2 Corinthians 10:5 back-to-back five or six times before I could gain control of my mind in that moment because thoughts would resurface immediately after I finished reading the verse! After a few days of frustration, I began reading the verses out loud and noticed that was a little more effective. But the nuisance had already set in. Thankfully, being a matter-of-fact person gave me the perseverance to buckle down and give it my best effort for longer than just a week! The Scripture says I can take *every* thought captive into the obedience of Christ, so *every* thought must be checked.

And sure enough, like everything else you set your mind to, I eventually started seeing the fruit of my labor and the breaking of a new day! I've gotten to the point where, out of sheer habit, I may address funky thoughts out loud. I won't hesitate to blurt out "nuh uhh" with a straight up attitude in my tone and facial expression! I try not to do this in public, of course, but I'm not overly conscious about it; if it happens, then it happens. I'm sure we've all experienced a neighbor on the bus, train, or while sitting in Starbucks or something utter an "umm" to themselves. Obviously, they're in their thoughts. Or maybe I'm just gracious in this area because that neighbor is probably me. But over the years, you can imagine how intolerant I've become of undesirable and/ or destructive thoughts that try to test me, looking to see if I'll choose to entertain them.

Most times I win, but sometimes I will absolutely get caught slipping! Recognizing when I'm venturing into this space comes much easier nowadays, but again, this could be a battle that never stops showing up at my doorstep. For instance, being in conflict with someone can trigger me. I'll begin daydreaming about the argument I had with the person, and I'll rewind and replay it just to see how many times I can change its outcome (in my favor, of course). If I find myself feeling offended by someone without having had an argument, I'll create in my mind how I think that argument would've gone. The goal of all this is to simply satisfy my flesh by fueling and indulging in whatever emotion I'm feeling. If I want to be upset, angry, or even enraged, I have the ability to indulge in that emotion through my imagination. If I'm feeling sadness or pain, I can indulge in those emotions as well, but I don't believe indulging in any of these negative emotions is for enjoyment— because they don't feel good. But what I *do* get is the ability to remain in my feelings. I get to allow my nature to remain in the space that is my reality, in that moment, only to find myself trapped in that state until something, someone, or the passing of time pulls me out of that mental and emotional prison.

I've finally learned how to consistently redirect my imagination when I daydream (if I choose to). This only came after completely turning it off for a while so I could focus on recalibrating and reprogramming my mind through the process of taking all my thoughts captive. I've been able to reclaim my mental stability and freedom, which happened to give me a taste of what it's like to control my emotions! It seems inadvertent, but I learned I can choose what I allow myself to feel, which is when I first tapped into the wisdom of not being ruled or governed by my emotions. I don't suppress my emotions by leaning more toward logic or anything like that. I'm able to walk this truth authentically by allowing myself to feel however I'm made to feel, but I know how to choose not to live in my feelings nor allow them to disable any of my other senses or faculties. I no longer have to allow my emotions to dictate to me via my perception, attitude, tone, behavior, etc.

Being a woman with a natural emotional bent is no longer a hall pass I carry around as an excuse to live, wallow in, or react out of my emotions. To feel hurt, offended, disappointed, angry, rejected, dismissed, or any cocktail of unpleasant emotions is not problematic, nor is it a sign of immaturity or weakness. I believe God created in women the ability to feel in the ways we do, so I imagine that to suppress how we feel is damaging. What I believe matters is how I allow myself to be impacted by what I feel and if I'll allow myself to wallow in the negative emotion(s) I'm legitimately experiencing. What matters is how I choose to engage and respond, and when I do, I'm usually way more measured and calculated, and oftentimes without much thought or preparation.

Going back to the basics, one of my new undertakings is to fill my mind with the thoughts God has for me as His child by going through the same exercise of taking my thoughts captive into the obedience of Christ and going to my colored index cards. My strategy hasn't changed much, except this time, being inspired by an exercise we did during a simulcast a few weeks ago, I'll write the Scripture verse verbatim and then paraphrase it on the back of the card.

A Favorite Psalm

I believe that most people find it hard to simply have a change of mind when it comes to our perspective on the simplest of matters, but a far more challenging undertaking is pivoting on what we believe. Being at the end of ourselves can push us toward the cliff, but taking the leap off the cliff is sometimes inconceivable. We can easily spend years sitting at the edge of the cliff! I've had my share of years sitting at mine, but after I decided to finally go for it the first time, leaping from it over and over gets easier and easier. I have chosen to believe that when I leap, God will not fail in causing the net to appear, and although I don't yet believe *everything* He says about me as His child, I've still chosen to leap. This is the only way I'll arrive to that place in my heart.

My very first group of verses are coming from my all-time favorite book and chapter in the Bible. I'm going line by line, writing and meditating on each individual verse until the sentiment of God's heart expressed throughout the chapter sticks.

"You have searched me, Lord, and you know me." (Ps 139:1)

Meditating on this verse began stimulating me emotionally. It redirected my heart toward God in a way that allowed me to connect with Him in a very meaningful way because of how it coincides with the reshaping and redefining of fatherhood. I really connect with the idea of Him knowing me because I come from Him, and I appreciate the way these two concepts overlap.

"You know when I sit and when I rise; you perceive my thoughts from afar." (Ps 139:2)

Repeatedly reciting this verse (both in my head and out loud) forces me to think on the Lord in a way that makes Him much closer to me than I've ever taken the time to imagine. It forces me to use the vivid imagination He gifted to me, but for purposes that benefit and push me closer to Him and the truth of who and how He is. When I meditate on this verse, it sends me back to His loving and kind discipline, where I felt like He was sitting on the side of my bed with me, reasoning with me, with his hand resting gently on the small of my back.

As I'm growing disciplined in doing this, I can see how I'm successfully forming the habit of placing God where He belongs and desires to be—where His virtues, thoughts, feelings, actions, and reputation sit at the forefront of my mind. I'm not yet fully consistent, but I feel that my progress is what allows me to see this as a success already. God is no longer at the center of my constant barrage of accusations against His character, although I still have moments where I do look at Him sideways. I still have times where I tap into fears about how He seems willing to let me down. But I'm becoming much more balanced and am shifting in the right direction. And I also have at the forefront of my mind the actual forces (carnality and demonic) behind my constant need to accuse God and sit in the judgment seat that always found Him guilty of whatever charge I levied against Him.

It has taken a very long time to completely silence the thoughts that fueled feelings of rejection, abandonment, unworthiness, vulnerability, and the idea that I didn't mean as much to God as I actually do. This silence isn't permanent because, like I said, Satan has no chill; he's always crouching at my door. But I'm now able to see the fruit of replacing the thoughts that needed to be silenced with the spiritual and biblical truths that reflect through a well-nourished spirit.

Chapter 10

Controversial Forgiveness

I'm sure you've noticed a common thread throughout my life that's also reflected among these pages, which is the power of my choice and its necessity in every area of my life. Forgiveness falls neatly within that reality. As far as I'm concerned, forgiveness has nothing to do with a feeling but everything to do with being an act of will to release me from the torment of someone else's words or actions perpetrated against me (or my perception of a person's wrongdoing). Choosing to forgive is choosing to no longer hold grudges or seek revenge and vindication for wrong(s) a person commits against me. Ironically, when I choose to forgive and not seek revenge or vindication for myself, I'm going completely against my temperament and natural inclination! I've never been one to hold grudges because I've always been on the opposite end of the spectrum. Before salvation, revenge was something that always gave me a sense of peace and satisfaction that always allowed me to continue being in a relationship with whoever was the culprit. Things as simple as refusing to give a friend a ride because of something they did or said (or didn't do), finding ways to damage a person's property, or cheating on a boyfriend are all things I've done without batting an eye.

When I became a believer, obviously I had to change my way of thinking and how I responded, so I ended up swinging to the other end of the spectrum until I learned how to release offenses and my perception of a person's "crime" and/or mistreatment of me. Many of us understand and are even well versed in the Scriptures relating to the command to forgive and all the associated benefits of forgiveness. Books and articles from both the religious and secular sectors are plentiful, with all kinds of ways forgiveness is profitable for the human soul. But so many of us still wrestle with forgiveness and often come out on the losing end. The shock for me is that many of us within the religious community struggle with unforgiveness and fail in ways that seem just as bad as those not within the community of faith. And no matter how hard we try, it's sometimes an impossible feat, and one we are rarely capable of or willing to admit as we pridefully hold on to the memories of the events and circumstances. We find creative and effective ways of coping with the unforgiveness lodged in our soul as we continue in our daily lives, not realizing the extent of how deeply we are affected. We overlook the different ways unforgiveness, like everything else, seeps out and kisses everything we touch, and even manifests in our bodies through sicknesses and ailments doctors would never be capable of getting to the root of (stress, headaches, stomach and digestive problems, etc.).

In my opinion, the type of forgiveness that is closer to being biblical is very unconventional and uncommon, especially within our society and culture. We dislike the idea that Scripture may actually instruct us to allow ourselves to be, what feels like, taken advantage of. I don't hear much preaching from verses like Matthew 18:21–22, where Peter asks Jesus how many times we should forgive our brother/sister, suggesting up to seven times, but Jesus turns around and ups the ante with 70 x 7! So, you mean to tell me you want me to forgive the person who keeps sinning against me *four hundred and ninety times*?!

In Luke 6:29, Jesus mentions that if a person slaps you, turn your other cheek toward them so they can slap that one too! And if someone wants the coat off your back, go on and give them your shirt too! Frankly, with my saved, sanctified, Holy Ghost-filled self, I can't tell you how many times I've given the Holy Spirit the screw-face with scrunched eyebrows when I read these passages. I stay away from these verses, too! I've never taken the time to pull out my different resources so I can dig into the cultural context of these verses, and what they meant back then, in order to apply them to my life today. I'm just not ready for that. And I'm certainly not complaining about the lack of preaching on these verses and topics (within the circles and spheres of influence I'm familiar with) because I don't know if I'm willing to be held to that high of a standard yet!

But what I have been able to reach, and not easily, is the standard of forgiving *and* forgetting. Forgiving and forgetting is another dynamic that's highly opposed and criticized, even among Christians. And I don't mean to be so hard on the Christian community, but in many ways I just expect more because of who (Jesus) and what (the Bible) we as believers are supposed to be led by. There are some areas in life that I believe we should be pros in, or at least have a good grip on. We are definitely just as broken as the unbeliever sitting beside us, but we personally know the wisest and most powerful person that exists, and His Spirit abides within us. We have access to supernatural strength, power, and authority, along with various tools specifically intended to help us conquer anything and everything that steps to us sideways. I certainly like making room for the fact that we all have to grow into spiritual maturity, and it happens over time as we grow at various paces, but I still feel there is an intense opposition to many things that, at least in my opinion, shouldn't necessarily be opposed.

In my experience, when I bring up the idea that the epitome of forgiveness is the decision to also forget, people love to argue me down with explanations that range from the fact that God gave us a memory for a reason, and remembering helps to protect from future and perpetual harm, to the fact that God doesn't forget our sins, and He never explicitly commands us to forgive and forget. I've had a number of these conversations throughout the years, both privately and publicly, and I completely understand these different positions most people hold and all their varying reasons for refusing to forget any of the offenses, betrayals and trauma stemming from perpetrators. I've held many of those beliefs myself at one time or another, but as I continue to dive deeper in my healing journey, the Holy Spirit is continually reshaping and shifting my perspective, and this is one of those areas where I can see my quality of life increasing.

The concept of forgiving *and* forgetting came primarily as a result of conflict within my marriage. Too often, I found myself being able to remember my husband's offenses and failures and the heartache that came with it. Whenever triggered by something, I'd often replay the circumstances and arguments in my mind that may have happened weeks or even months earlier. There were many times where—after I completed the work of forgiving my husband and moved forward—a new conflict that felt familiar to the old one would trigger me, and all those old feelings attached to the old and resolved conflict resurfaced and further complicated the new one. I hated being back at square one and having to do double work of re-releasing the old situation and release the new clash. I had to work through a new cocktail of emotions that folded into the old.

This was exhausting for both of us because sometimes I needed my husband's help to work through and patch up everything. And you can imagine, he had his own difficulties in those instances where we found ourselves having to agree to disagree on certain principles while making arrangements and commitments for the sake of peace within the marriage and household. At times, I felt embarrassed that these old feelings resurfaced, and shame would rise at the possibility that I deceived myself into thinking I forgave my husband and moved on when that may not have been the case. The sense of pride I felt for having the maturity and grace to forgive and move on would evaporate because I was doing the total opposite of what I had intended. I hate being self-deceived. I hate walking in falsehood and deception.

Thankfully, my husband was extremely loving and understanding; he was very gracious toward me during these times and even appreciated my willingness and courage to bring my vulnerability and frailness to him. Talk about being a burden-bearer for me! And, although I was grateful to my husband, I was also extremely tired of these do-overs. It didn't make sense to be in such close proximity to another human who was as prone to his humanity as I am, and to live out the rest of my life constantly having these repeated issues that carried so much emotional baggage with them. Hebrews 8:12 came to mind:

> "For I will forgive their wickedness
> and will remember their sins no more."

It dawned on me that perhaps I can follow God's example of no more remembering past offenses. Just forget about them altogether. I prayed a simple but fervent and heartfelt prayer, asking the Holy Spirit to allow me the freedom to no longer remember anything I choose to forget after I've released forgiveness. Within the most significant earthly relationship I have, it just made perfect sense. Not one reason under the sun could be good enough to hold my husband hostage to the memory of his past mistakes, offenses, and failures (let alone my perception of his mistakes, offenses, and failures). The greater good of our marriage couldn't be served when remembering the circumstances and emotions surrounding past conflicts.

When attempting to have and maintain a Christ-centered marriage, there is absolutely no room for this mentality or behavior. I'll look at my husband now and automatically feel, *He doesn't deserve to be held hostage for the mistakes he made one, two, or even seven years ago. He doesn't deserve anything less than the freedom that comes from not having anything being held over his head relating to our past.* That's not love. The very fabric of our marital relationship could be destroyed, and I didn't want that. So, when I decide to forgive, forgetting comes with it. When a conflict or set of circumstances prove challenging to forget, prayer is my go-to as I ask the Holy Spirit for His help in forgetting. Like clockwork, He comes through every single time. It's to the point where I wish I could remember some of our past conflicts when in conversations with other couples, but I can't for the life of me recall anything. It can be frustrating at times because so many conflicts in marriage are similar across the board, and we really enjoy helping younger couples struggling in the same (or similar) areas we've struggled. And it's so refreshing sharing our experiences with a peer or more seasoned couples. But I am not frustrated enough to forgo not being able to remember! For the sake of my peace and the preservation of the fabric of my marriage, that stuff can remain in the abyss, and if ever I feel led, I'll ask the Lord to bring things back to my remembrance. But so far I've not felt led to do any of that, and that request has not been made!

Having cultivated this within my marital relationship enables me to carry it over into every other relationship and friendship. I've been able to free up a profound amount of mental and emotional real estate, and the quality of my relationships and interactions has increased astronomically. When people say they have forgiven but won't forget, I find the most common reason is their need to protect themselves from being hurt again or repeatedly taken advantage of. Somehow, remembering the offenses, recalling the circumstances, and keeping tabs on the hurt and heartache equates to providing the wisdom necessary to prevent being taken advantage of and hurt repeatedly by an offender. I counter that logic with the idea that one doesn't need to remember a situation or any of the details surrounding the conflict in order to pull the lesson learned and apply the wisdom gained to future interactions—with the offender or people in general.

The lesson(s) learned and the wisdom gained stand on their own. They will likely become a part of who we are and how we operate moving forward; they will inform our future interactions and the decision we make as it relates to distancing ourselves from folks and even removing certain individuals from our lives altogether. We don't have to recall the pain suffered in an attempt to use it as a buffer or to control our surroundings and protect our hearts. Letting go of *everything* frees us in such significant ways, and it releases us from the emotional stress we don't even realize is floating beneath the surface, informing how we operate within our interactions with others. We can absolutely take the "face" off the lesson and disconnect and remove the circumstances from the wisdom and insight we receive from these unfortunate experiences. Let the lesson, the clarity, and the wisdom stand on their own. Then apply them as we see fit moving forward.

In some instances, holding on and choosing to remember everything only serves the purpose of having ammunition in our arsenal. When dealing with family, friends, and people in general, but particularly those who are in close proximity, it can mean everything to be fully locked, loaded, and ready to fire on our opponent when the past resurfaces. Having the "facts" of the situation on our hip, recalling what was said and done, remembering how we felt in the moments of our conflict, etc. are all invaluable to us during these heated and often emotional exchanges. When the goal is to be right and win or to defend and justify ourselves or to just crush our "adversary" within that particular quarrel, having the ability to recall every detail serves up a level of power and muscle that helps to dominate in ways only the flesh will revel in.

But in any relationship that's meaningful, the other party is never our enemy or adversary. When communicating and discussing a problem, the ultimate objective is to resolve the issue! The goal is to clear the air and settle the dispute so we can get back to relating in an atmosphere of love, kindness, joy, and peace. I have found that the easiest way to return to the bliss of our relationship or friendship is the ability to forgive and forget, allowing them to be attached to one another. So far, they have not failed me. And I'm in conflict often, which is not something I'm bragging about; it's just a part of my nature to be confrontational (in the eyes of some) because I don't run from or avoid conflict, I engage. It's a skill that's cultivated over time, but the key to all relationships is to know how to resolve conflict. My richest and most healthy relationships are with those that have tackled conflict and fought with me to overcome the tension within our relationship—which is always my ultimate goal. I don't see any reason why two or more people who are in relationship shouldn't be able to resolve any conflict that arises—especially within the community of believers. Being the black and white person that I am, I find the Scriptures to be very clear in how we are to resolve disagreements, and it's really just a matter of doing what the Bible says. Plain and simple.

In conflicts where forgiveness proves too difficult to release, I'll ask the Holy Spirit to help me forget the details surrounding the conflict first so I can then move toward releasing forgiveness. Perhaps this is easy for me since it was never in my nature to remember and hold on to offenses. Granted, the reason behind that (being vengeful) isn't virtuous or honorable, but it may have cultivated the ability to forget more easily than others. Either way it doesn't matter how it comes or how I get it, being liberated in my mind and emotions is a by-any-means necessary type of situation. I've tasted the fruit, and I do not want to partake in anything rotted anymore.

Chapter 11

The Church: Inadvertently Complicit

O ne of my biggest concerns with being critical of the church is the imbalance that can often come with it. As with anything, you can place the spotlight on the issues that clearly need attention and should be addressed while being unaware—or not fully understanding—of some of its root causes. This can cause any assessment to be riddled with holes, as a result of pure ignorance, while rendering the plight to find realistic solutions unproductive and/or not applicable. My desire and intention are to be balanced in my approach as I share my personal observations and perspective on a topic that affects me personally, while also understanding my limitations. I'm not aware of, nor have I visited, a significant number of churches spread across the United States; in fact, I'm not even aware of just how many exist and what they're all doing with their congregations and surrounding communities. Additionally, I'm not even savvy with statistics concerning American churches, church life, etc.

Ironically, what I'm describing reminds me of racism and systemic oppression in America, whereby most people who are not scholars or experts on the topic, no matter what side they sit on, can be deeply uninformed, misinformed, and flat out unqualified to not only assess but also formulate solutions that could actually have an impact on the number of layers to the issues African Americans face on a day-to-day basis. Even those of us directly impacted by oppression and racism have a very small lens through which we view the overall big picture (and many/most white people are at a much higher disadvantage because of their lack of experience, interaction with black people, and understanding of the numerous issues that plague generations of African Americans). Ignorance is ignorance. And I'm fully aware of my non-exempt status.

So, in no way am I approaching or attempting to address the church as a theologian, expert, or scholar of the Bible, church, or religious life. It is not my intention to "school" anyone about the overall state of the church; I'm simply sharing my perspective on how fatherlessness doesn't appear to be an issue that's receiving the attention from many of the churches that I'm familiar with, and my assumption is that this could be the case for possibly most. I believe this could be part of the reason why fatherlessness and its effects continue to be an epidemic plaguing society which is flowing directly into our pews and even behind the pulpit! And, to be clear, when I talk about "the church" I am primarily talking about the religious institution, the organization, and its culture, not necessarily the church as in the Body and Bride of Christ.

Going it Alone

Church culture and the clichés that float around go hand in hand. For the most part, I've reached a point where I don't care one bit for either of them, clichés especially. I'll concede that very few carry some substance, but most others, by my estimation, are pure foolishness. For instance, one day while out and about with my mom running errands, she said in the midst of one of our conversations, "God blesses fools and babies." If only you could have seen my face when I heard that come out of her mouth, as if she had just quoted John 3:16. I turned toward her and asked, "Soooo what about people like me?" All she could do was laugh, and granted it was indeed a light moment, but my gosh, hearing stuff like that pour out of the mouths of Christians can really burn me up. I've been pushed to the point of hating about 90% of clichés that are typical within church culture. I don't want to hear clichés; just quote the Bible! But of the 10% that don't bother me or do carry a message that resonates with me, I appreciate the message beneath that actually makes sense. One example is the admonishment to "know who you are in Christ."

The truth sitting underneath that phrase has the potential to spur action in a believer who realizes they can't answer the question, "Do you know who you are in Christ?" I remember when I couldn't answer that question in the affirmative, and I can also recall when that changed. It came after I spent time reading the Bible and accumulating the different Scriptures that helped me discover and define my identity in Christ. My identity was reinforced through the time I spent in corporate worship, sitting under solid preaching and teaching through the years. However, my identity was locked up within knowing who I am as a believer, follower, and lover of Jesus Christ; being a servant of the Lord; and being an ambassador in the earth—but not necessarily as His child.

I'm on that same path where I'm reading the Bible and being intentional with accumulating and examining the Scriptures so I can embrace what the Lord says about me as His beloved daughter. Only this time I'm doing this completely alone. I don't have the reinforcement I had through the corporate worship experience because it's not an issue that's addressed on a regular basis (within my region or over the airwaves, such as YouTube, radio stations, podcasts, etc., that I frequent). Over the more than fifteen years that I've been a believer and avid churchgoer, I can't recall fatherlessness being addressed over the pulpit, in Bible study or during growth group meetings on a continual basis. A sermon here and there or a series at one point every couple of years isn't enough; that's nothing more than a small rain shower over a dried-up lake, as far as I'm concerned. The awareness being sprinkled around is inconsequential, and no real change can begin to take place in the hearts and minds of those of us within the four walls of the church; this lack of change doesn't have the ability to spill out and flow into communities and begin the process of influencing the culture and shifting society in the right direction. There doesn't seem to be any true ministries that specifically aim to serve the fatherless on a grand scale, like we do the homeless or the incarcerated for example.

There are a few handfuls of church leaders and ministries that I'm personally aware of (through my readings) that have etched the issue of fatherlessness into the foundation of their ministry. But for some reason, this hasn't hit the church like the wildfire or firestorm it should. I can't help but wonder how we are all, on some level, familiar with the significance of this issue. There are a large number of us both sitting in the pew and standing behind the pulpit who are personally affected by this—yet we are watching generation after generation continue in this same cycle of father absence.

Let's Start Somewhere

I can't help but wonder what the reason behind this phenomenon could be. Why are church leaders seemingly overlooking the necessity of placing this epidemic at the forefront of ministry and service to our congregations? How are we continuing to neglect one of the most basic and fundamental needs of the single-family homes that often make up large portions of congregations in some communities? Surely the church should have by now come to the place of addressing and resolving the problem of absent men who have the responsibility of being, as Dr. Myles Munroe puts it, the very foundation and anchor of everything— his home, marriage, family, church and ministry, community, and ultimately culture and society. Granted, there may not be a lot that can be done immediately in the way of pulling these men and fathers into the church, but we can at least start somewhere by recognizing and acknowledging the absence to the degree that we mobilize the men and fathers that *are* present. We have to start somewhere, so why not begin with the current generation of youth (and maybe even young adults) who are now presently filling our churches?!

In *The Fatherhood Principle*, Dr. Myles Munroe said something that has always echoed in my heart, but I could never put it together as nicely as he has:.

> "If the male doesn't hold like an anchor, society goes adrift and crashes on the rocks of immorality and broken values, and we lose the vision and destiny of the country and the programs and resources of the community. Everything falls apart when the anchor isn't holding." [8]

I honestly believe that the foundation of our society stands on the spiritual principles of men and fatherhood, and the many ills of our society and the constant decline of our culture and morale are a mere reflection of the disintegrating foundation and anchor of our nation—our men. In no way am I minimizing the role of women and mothers and the impact we've had through the decades, both holding society together while simultaneously advancing it forward. But neither men nor women were purposed to do anything alone or apart from one another. We are designed and purposed to work together, hand in hand, with the same level of partnership required to procreate. And I fervently agree with Dr. Munroe's thought when he describes the purpose of males from a biblical perspective:

> Understanding the purpose for the male is a critical and necessary step in understanding fatherhood, because the male was designated (*design*-ated) a father by the Creator. God was thinking "father" when He created man. As a matter of fact, buried in every boy is the potential of being a father. This means that God intends for every boy to grow up into fatherhood. Again, I am not just talking about the male's biological ability to father offspring. Being a "father" is rooted in God's image because God

---

8 Myles Munroe, *The Fatherhood Principle* (New Kensington: Whitaker House, 2008) p. 186.

is Father. He is not satisfied until the father comes out of the boy. Fatherhood is the design and destiny of the male.[9]

Across the board, the churches I'm familiar with, no matter the denomination, have and maintain several types of ministries that both aim to fulfill the different needs of the congregation and/or focus on addressing specific issues that afflict the communities they serve. We all have our deacon and deaconess boards, missionaries, and evangelists; we have our music ministry, men's ministry, women's ministry, youth and young adult ministry, and children's ministry; we have various forms of outreach ministries, such as the prison ministry and the homeless ministry; we can't forget our singles, so we have our singles' ministry and their upgrade to the marriage ministry. Depending on the location of the church, its surrounding community, and the specific makeup of the congregation, we start to see different types of worship and arts ministries, college ministries, creative ministries for youth and young adults, ministries for recreation, etc.

These ministries are the lifeblood of the church, hands down, and I personally wouldn't want it any other way. There's nothing that can come close to the fulfillment and satisfaction of having so many different options and having the ability to plug in to and participate in different ministries that help develop relationships and friendships. There's not much that can compare to being a part of a vibrant and growing church family.

God's Perspective

Only recently, within the last few years, have I grown into the understanding that the church, as in *the Body of Christ*, has the very purpose and calling to father the fatherless. We are distinctively equipped to address and reduce the issue of father absence and the varying problems

---

9 Ibid., p. 25–26.

and evils attached to it. And since we are purposed and called to this work, we possess the power and the know-how to bring forth the awareness, correction, education, and training that can facilitate and bring forth the healing, restoration, growth, and development of those of us who pile into the church building week after week. We have the authority and the ability to help families without men, or fathers, assimilate into the family of God in ways that are far more meaningful than just being a churchgoer who inevitably sits on the outskirts of a relationship with the Lord as a present and active father in their lives. It's not enough to just be believers of Jesus Christ, filled with the Holy Spirit, serving the one true living God. He's so much more to us than that.

Plain and simple, God is not okay with disregarding the fatherless in any way, shape, or form. He is extremely clear in how He feels about the fatherless and what He desires for the fatherless through the hands and resources of the surrounding community. I only want to highlight two verses (I've included almost thirty in appendix A):

> "A father to the fatherless, a defender of widows, is God in his holy dwelling. God sets the lonely in families, He leads out the prisoners with singing; but the rebellious live in a sun-scorched land." (Ps 68:5–6, emphasis mine)

> "Religion that God our Father accepts as pure and faultless is this: to look after orphans and widows in their distress and to keep oneself from being polluted by the world." (Jas 1:27)

Throughout Scripture we, the body of believers, are admonished in our role to be a true community to the families affected by fatherlessness. God is black and white on this issue and made it a point throughout the Bible to speak on His expectations of His people to ensure care, concern, compassion, and justice for the fatherless (and those who are less fortunate). These various stipulations throughout the Bible were not given to the Israelites for information purposes, He intended for them to be imitated.[10]

By my estimation, not only do we have a gap in the church that we keep overlooking but we may be at the threshold of flat out neglecting something God is clear about and expects us to address. We may have even crossed over the threshold already, especially since we often carry a pride and arrogance about ourselves when we feel we've "arrived," despite the many challenges and difficulties that can torment fatherless children. Fatherless children grow up to be dysfunctional adults, often not realizing the dysfunction nor understanding why. We can so often bend toward the notion that "I grew up without my biological father and I'm doing and will continue to be just fine," and I've heard many peers echo the sentiment that they never needed their father in the first place.

It's long overdue for the issues of fatherlessness to be brought to the forefront, addressed consistently, and placed in priority alongside evangelism, outreach, fundraising, and the music ministry. It is *our* responsibility and calling. Tim Beilharz put it perfectly:

> We cannot simply abdicate this responsibility to schools or government agencies. While these organizations are essential, we the church are called to provide and care for the fatherless in our community as a mark of God's justice in the world. We need to provide male role models, spiritual fathers and grandfathers to these young boys and young girls, and provide safe ministry structures in which these relationships can take place. In doing so we model the loving, justice-upholding fatherhood of God to these young children. [11]

---

10 Mark E. Strong, *Church for the Fatherless* (Downers Grove: InterVarsity Press, 2012), p. 63.

11 Tim Beilharz, "Fathering the Fatherless in Our Churches," GoThereFor.com (website), accessed January 21, 2016, http://gotherefor.com/offer.php?intid=29169.

Moving Forward

Apostle Paul in 1 Corinthians 4 models the responsibility of being a spiritual father, and I believe men in the church should be looking for young men and women, boys, and girls they can spiritually adopt and father. The majority of them (us) with absent fathers are longing for this in our lives, and oftentimes we don't realize it ourselves. We're simply trying to make the best of life with what we have to work with. And, to be frank, no shade toward mentoring programs—because they can be excellent vehicles—but I believe a mentor and a spiritual father are drastically different in that spiritual fathers have a higher level of responsibility and investment into the everyday lives of those they are fathering. Spiritual fathers are (usually) more vested than mentors and carry a higher level of intimacy and closeness with the family overall. And we need to ensure the least of us have the same opportunities to be fathered, not just the incredibly gifted, talented, and anointed preacher or musician coming up in the faith.

To tackle fatherlessness in our churches means we will have a greater effect when it comes to evangelizing the community and the city, ultimately shifting society. To mobilize the men of the church may ignite the faithful, enthusiastic service of men, setting them free into their purpose and passion to be the men and fathers of the community—the way God desires and has always intended. Scott Mac-Naughton co-founded a church-based organization called Fathers in the Field, and through his program, his deacons had their biblical roles returned to them, which is caring for the widows and the fatherless. Their organization is primarily geared toward filling the gap for the boys in their churches, and he says that these youngsters aren't the only ones changed. The experience transforms the church as the widows, and single mothers, have become front and center of their ministry. They are now being pursued, as the men of the church are constantly helping and finding ways to meet their needs, while the other women in the church dive into service as a natural response of our compassionate nature.[12]

Dr. Mark E. Strong's book *Church for the Fatherless: A Ministry Model for Society's Most Pressing Problem* is an excellent resource and starting point for churches and ministries because he speaks from the experience of his own ministry. At the time he was planting Life Change Church in Portland, Oregon, he noticed that about 75% of his leadership didn't have fathers in their lives. This became his mission, and his book outlines a number of very practical ways he was able to make a difference. In a nutshell, I pulled the following skeleton from his book:

Embed the value of fathering the fatherless among the leadership of the church on a consistent and regular basis by a) creating an awareness, b) creating significant avenues for ministry, and c) celebrating and rewarding progress in meaningful ways because the undertaking is enormous.[13]

1) Use the vehicle of preaching to mobilize and equip the congregation for the ministry of serving the fatherless.[14]

2) Begin equipping the men in the church to be exceptional fathers to their own families.[15]

3) Pray fervently over the endeavor, the ministry, the leaders, and the people.

4) To say the least, I'm not suggesting this is a walk in the park, but I am suggesting that the church currently may be complicit without meaning to be, and we need to finally start moving forward.

---

12 Megan Fowler, "Fighting for the Fatherless: Changing Lives, Transforming Churches," BYFAITH MAGAZINE (website), accessed May 8, 2013, https://byfaithonline.com/fighting-for-the-fatherless-2/.

13 Strong, *Church for the Fatherless*, p. 64–68.

14 Ibid., p. 74–78; 109–111.

15 Ibid., p. 95–102.

Epilogue

*A*fter initial contact with my biological father, he and I kept in touch by phone over the next few years. It didn't take long for my heart to begin softening toward him, and a genuine love and affection between us began to sprout. I can't readily pinpoint it, but my outlook on life felt a little different just having the ability to say that I had a father that I called every now and then to chat with. But it wasn't anything significant or life changing. More than anything, it just felt good, especially since it came just a couple of years before my new dad (Daniel Thornton) showed up on the scene. But interestingly enough, my fondness and acceptance of Gerry really took root once I developed a father-daughter relationship with my dad. True to his nature, my dad made it a point to gently nudge me toward a relationship with Gerry. My dad was effective in filling all my empty pits that fatherlessness created while diligently reconstructing the collapsed bridge that currently allows me to reach God in this new context. I'm finally experiencing Him as my ultimate Father.

My husband and I eventually relocated from Washington, DC, back to my hometown of Pittsburgh, and I expected my relationship with Gerry to take off. But the needle of our relationship hardly moved. In addition to reaching out to him by phone every now and then, the culture of his home was to just stop by because someone would always be home. So that's what I did, and sure enough, someone was always home! It was pretty nice being around him and his family, even when he wasn't around. I was able to nurture my relationship with my younger sister and brothers. Ms. Dina treated me with a loving-kindness that allowed me to feel like I wasn't just a part of the family; I felt she and I were almost friends. Gerry always gushed over me, as he constantly wanted to reminisce about the good old times between him and my mother and worked to bring me up to speed regarding his side of the family.

Unfortunately, Gerry never really took an interest in getting to know me. He rarely inquired about my life and side of history. While with me, he always lived in the past and our conversations were always very one-sided. In hindsight, this was and is so disappointing. I imagined he would have taken somewhat of an interest in me, but he never asked me about my childhood, high school experiences, or college. Through the years, he never asked what I did for a living and didn't take an interest in my husband or how we met or if we planned to have children.

While appreciating the time I got to spend with him, it took a while for me to realize and acknowledge the imbalance. He wasn't putting forth much effort to call me to check in and see how I was doing or what I was up to. Of the ten years I had been back in Pittsburgh, he only stopped by my home once. I invited him and his family to my vow renewal ceremony and loved that they came, but my dad is the one who had the honor of walking me down the aisle and re-presenting me to my husband. Reconnecting with Gerry so many years prior to my ceremony could have been an opportunity for him to have earned the privilege of walking me down the aisle, but all he earned was the invitation for him and his family to be present—which as far as I'm concerned, was pretty big. I only had a guest list of about fifty *close* family and friends.

Finally, I decided to call him and ask why he doesn't keep in touch with me. He talked about my phone number always changing, preventing him from staying in closer contact with me, and I assured him my number was still the same, but not much changed. By the third mention to him regarding his lack of effort, I was no longer casually bringing this up; I was calling him to the carpet. Him using the same excuse prompted me to have him grab his phone and call the number he had programmed in his address book, and sure enough, my phone rang in my purse as I sat at his infamous dining room table! Without giving him a hard time, I managed to make my point clear because I noticed he seemed a little embarrassed and at a loss for words. I didn't want this to become an issue, but it needed to be addressed, and he needed to know that I wasn't the type of person he could say anything to while I act like everything is okay. I engage to get to the root of things so they can be resolved. Things still didn't change much.

I decided to take a step back and see if he would begin putting forth effort toward getting to know me and actually building a relationship that wasn't centered around him. We became friends on Facebook, but we rarely interacted with one another, except on two occasions. Both were unpleasant. On the first interaction, he assumed a post I made was about him. He commented and we had an interesting exchange where I ultimately explained to him that not only was he incorrect in his assumption about my post but he also didn't know me well enough to say some of the things he said. A day later, he sent me an inbox message explaining that he reread my post and apologized for his misunderstanding. I really appreciated that gesture; it meant a lot to me. We then went back to the way things were, where he didn't reach out to me and I didn't reach out to him.

Fast forward about two years, where the development of this book began to take shape. Throughout my writing journey, I freely shared my thoughts and feelings about the writing process, memories I recalled, and even excerpts from the book. While editing and polishing the first chapter, I found myself smiling and feeling good about the initial interaction we had when I saw him for the first time face-to-face back in 2002, so I took a quick break, opened up Facebook and went to his timeline. I wrote, "I'm in the process of writing my book and am editing a chapter detailing the first time I saw you (as an adult). Just wanted to come over and say hello. Hope you're doing well." I left a heart emoji at the end. To my surprise, he was under the false impression that this book was about him personally. He assumed I was writing a novel that would essentially drag him out into the open, sullying his name and reputation, and he responded to my post with a long, scathing comment that was not only offensive but insulted me in a number of different ways.

Epilogue

Despite the reality of his comment and the things he said, I didn't take immediate offense. I was definitely shocked but I simply recognized that he didn't know the actual topic and content of this book. I tried taking the high road. I didn't address anything he said in his comment; I only responded with how great my family and I were doing (not that he asked), told him the ages of my sons, and that we were expecting again (details he didn't know); and I reiterated that I was writing and preparing to launch my book and hoped he'd support it, but if not, I understood (which is true). I finished by telling him to take care of himself and tell everyone I said hello. My mission in taking the high road was complete! I refrained from entertaining his inappropriate, insensitive, ill-informed initial response that was laced with insults. After the shock of that situation, I was able to recover and spend the rest of the day unbothered.

However, the next morning when I woke up . . . .

The moment I opened my eyes, I began to rage in my heart as I recalled how I actually felt while reading his comment on my post. I began to fume, and by the time my feet touched the floor, it was decided that I would be paying him a visit. Immediately.

I went downstairs and greeted and talked with my husband briefly, greeted my boys, got dressed and was in my car on my way to his house. The purpose and goal of my visiting him was three-fold: I wanted to understand where he was coming from and why he responded the way he did, address how it made me feel, and bring some clarity to him regarding the purpose and subject of my book. I wanted to clear the air by coming to a mutual understanding surrounding facts and truth. By the time I arrived at his home, my fuming was long gone because I genuinely desired and fully expected to have a productive conversation that would end with everything settled between the two of us. My demeanor and disposition reflected that I was serious, but I was still pleasant and cordial. When I arrived at his home and made my way up to him, he actually lit up and greeted me very pleasantly, as if nothing had transpired between us on a public social platform. I appreciated his greeting because it reassured me that we wouldn't be going to war with words.

To say the least, the conversation didn't go well. At all! When we got into the thick of things, Gerry refused to answer some of the simplest questions, which bothered me to the point where I was beginning to lose respect for him. While ranting, he revealed some of the offenses he had been accruing and managed to lob a few more accusations and insults my way. Trying to remain respectful, I expressed to him that if this was how the conversation was going to continue, I would gladly leave. He decided that was the best course of action, and he essentially kicked me out of his home.

When I got back into my car, the nature and stress of that interaction with him was crushing. The experience was nowhere near what I had intended, and the way he rose up against me, considering how mild mannered he is, caught me completely off guard. I was shaking from the experience as I got into my car and inserted my key into the ignition. On one hand, the heaviness of that interaction—riding on the heels of the conflict being on Facebook in response to me simply saying hello—made me want to pull off with tears streaming down my face. On the other hand, being a vlogger caused me to pull out my camera and record myself in order to capture the reality of the situation, especially since I believed the situation would be diffused without too many hiccups.

In many ways, I blame myself because I should have been prepared and much more realistic about how our interaction *could* go, since he had already shown me his propensity to make assumptions, draw his own conclusions without having a conversation first, and be completely convinced of what he has decided to be truth. To some degree there was a glimmer of hope because he has also shown himself to be reasonable per our first altercation on Facebook, where he reassessed everything and was humble enough to apologize. But that apology came after his misperception of something that had nothing to do with him personally. This time, he was crystal clear about what he thought about me. It hurt deeply. I believed and expected more of him, while not aware of how little he thought of me. Without praying, I decided I'd be severing all ties with Gerry. But the door will always be open for reconciliation. If ever he reached out to me and wanted to talk, meet, or see his grandsons, etc., I will oblige without hesitation. But, he will have to be the one to initiate this and put forth the effort.

When I reached home, I shared the shock and awe of the conversation with my husband, and we chatted about it for a little while. Hunger crept in and I warmed up a plate of pancakes and sausage that my husband cooked for the family (don't get it twisted, though; he is not in the kitchen holding it down by any stretch of the imagination).

I sat alone at the table, and a question suddenly bubbled up out of my spirit. "How do you feel?" I paused for a moment, realizing it was the Holy Spirit, and I answered internally, *I'm cool with everything.* I felt Him ask again, "But how do you feel?" So, I took a moment to assess how I really felt, and in the midst of my thoughts, tears began to stream down my cheeks. I decided to sit there and allow myself to really feel the disappointment and pain of the situation. While considering how I felt about the things Gerry said in his comment and while in his home, particularly the things he thought about me, all of a sudden, I was a little girl on the inside and couldn't understand how or why a father would think or say some of the things he said. Especially considering the reality that he didn't know me (or much about me) in any meaningful way.

At this point, I could feel the ugly-faced cry coming on. I'm talking about the Gizmogotwet-and-turned-into-a-gremlin-looking cry.

From the moment I left Gerry's home in 2002, I find it unbelievable that although my heart was still hardened, I was so willing to give him a clean slate. I never thought evil of him, never made assumptions about him that I didn't give him the opportunity to clarify, and never questioned his character or intentions. I chose to believe that he was a nice guy, a human prone to mistakes and failures like us all—one who made a few bad mistakes concerning me. But it wasn't ever in me to hold his mistakes and failures—as they related to me—against him. I asked him some tough questions and believed what he said. I gave him the benefit of the doubt, and I was genuinely interested in getting to know him. And he was given a clean and clear platform in my life to build upon as he chose.

During the time we did spend together, what could have possibly given him the impression that I was anything close to the person he believed me to be? At his age, how could he allow himself to be so wrapped up in his own confusion, and so full of misunderstandings and offenses—without clearing the air—to the degree that he would lash out at me like a wild and unruly bear? How dare he not offer or extend any of the grace toward me that I had extended to him? And how do you think so lowly of someone you barely know, despite our familial connection? Especially after all he *never* did for me!

I put my fork down, unable to finish my pancakes, and sat in my seat looking out the window directly ahead of me, gazing at the sky. When the tears finally finished, I felt that sense of relief and peace that can only come from such an intense soul cry. In my mind, I saw different choices surfacing for various questions that strolled by. How am I going to allow this to affect me moving forward? How am I going to allow this to affect the writing of my book? Should I retaliate in some way? Does this affect my healing journey? Will it cause me to regress in any way? How long will I hold onto the pain and memory of this situation? Should I put him on blast on social media? How about I just go back to the post and cybersmack him a few times!?

I made my way over to the couch, and my husband came over and sat next to me, reaching out and resting his hand on my leg. We sat quietly.

Epilogue

I came to the decision to chalk everything up to Gerry being in his humanity which exposed who he really is, his true character. His insults and accusations were nothing more than a mere reflection of him, his guilt, and his inability to cultivate a meaningful relationship with the adult daughter he didn't have the privilege of raising. And I can't afford to internalize anything he believes or has said. I decided nothing in this book would be re-edited in any way because of how accurately it depicts what happened, what I thought, and how I felt as I moved through the years. Forgiveness would be released and forgetting the circumstances is the name of the game.

Thankfully, this situation has had no impact on my journey and progress with experiencing the Lord as my present and active Father. I haven't regressed one bit. I am continuing to maneuver through the terrain of my relationship with Him with seasons where I still manage to swing like a pendulum between my evolving truth and His absolute truth, but progressing forward nonetheless—especially with having a dad who's always around and ready to pick up the pieces, no matter how jagged the edges may be.

I haven't arrived yet and I'm not ashamed about that. But I expect to arrive sooner than later, and with great anticipation, I can't wait to see what it's like to truly live in the fullness of God's love—to live loved!

May the Journey
Continue . . . .

*T*he road hasn't ended for me. I still have a good amount of progress to make, and I'm hoping those of you who can join me, will—because there's no reason why we should travel this path alone. I desire to build a community of women who can come together (physically and virtually) to inspire, encourage, strengthen, and grow as we dive deeper within our individual and collective relationships with the one, true Living God, who is and will always be a present and active Father.

In the coming months, I'll be looking to visit various churches in different cities with the specific goal of meeting with women similar to me, no matter where in our journey we find ourselves. I want to be a part of a lively and vibrant community of women who are authentically living within the splendor of the Father's love and who are anxiously looking for opportunities to celebrate our breakthroughs and milestones—together. There is an incredible and indescribable power that can reside within a community of women who care more about truth in the inward parts and value sincerity and transparency over pride, clichés and Christian cultural norms. I want to tap into that!

I'm laying the foundation; if you are into this kind of thing, join me in building this community! First, start sharing your story and use #LearningtoLiveLoved when posting on your preferred social media platforms. Start looking for that hashtag and make sure you connect with me and others who are doing the same thing.

Connect with me on Twitter and Facebook @iamdelmesha and Instagram @iam.delmesha. (Yes, they're whack for not having my handle available...one that's not even being used!) Also, feel free to connect via email at iamdelmesha@gmail.com.

Let's just show up!!

Appendix A

Scriptures on Fatherlessness16

Exodus 22:22 Do not take advantage of the widow or the fatherless.

Deuteronomy 10:18 He defends the cause of the fatherless and the widow, and loves the foreigner residing among you, giving them food and clothing.

Deuteronomy 14:28–29 At the end of every three years, bring all the tithes of that year's produce and store it in your towns, so that the Levites (who have no allotment or inheritance of their own) and the foreigners, the fatherless and the widows who live in your towns may come and eat and be satisfied, and so that the Lord your God may bless you in all the work of your hands.

Deuteronomy 24:17–21 Do not deprive the foreigner or the fatherless of justice, or take the cloak of the widow as a pledge. Remember that you were slaves in Egypt and the Lord your God redeemed you from there. That is why I command you to do this. When you are harvesting in your field and you overlook a sheaf, do not go back to get it. Leave it for the foreigner, the fatherless and the widow, so that the Lord your God may bless you in all the work of your hands. When you beat the olives from your trees, do not go over the branches a second time. Leave what remains for the foreigner, the fatherless and the widow. When you harvest the grapes in your vineyard, do not go over the vines again. Leave what remains for the foreigner, the fatherless and the widow.

Deuteronomy 26:12 When you have finished setting aside a tenth of all your produce in the third year, the year of the tithe, you shall give it to the Levite, the foreigner, the fatherless and the widow, so that they may eat in your towns and be satisfied.

---

16 Mark E. Strong, *Church for the Fatherless*, p. 176 (Appendix B).

Deuteronomy 27:19 Cursed is anyone who withholds justice from the foreigner, the fatherless or the widow. Then all the people shall say, "Amen!"

Job 29:11–12 Whoever heard me spoke well of me, and those who saw me commended me, because I rescued the poor who cried for help, and the fatherless who had none to assist them.

Psalm 10:14 But you, God, see the trouble of the afflicted; you consider their grief and take it in hand. The victims commit themselves to you; you are the helper of the fatherless.

Psalm 10:17–18 You, Lord, hear the desire of the afflicted; you encourage them, and you listen to their cry, defending the fatherless and the oppressed, so that mere earthly mortals will never again strike terror.

Psalm 68:5–6 A father to the fatherless, a defender of widows, is God in his holy dwelling. God sets the lonely in families, he leads out the prisoners with singing; but the rebellious live in a sunscorched land.

Psalm 82:3 Defend the weak and the fatherless; uphold the cause of the poor and the oppressed.

Psalm 146:9 The Lord watches over the foreigner and sustains the fatherless and the widow, but he frustrates the ways of the wicked.

Proverbs 23:10–11 Do not move an ancient boundary stone or encroach on the fields of the fatherless, for their Defender is strong; he will take up their case against you.

Isaiah 1:17 Learn to do right; seek justice. Defend the oppressed. Take up the cause of the fatherless; plead the case of the widow.

Isaiah 10:1–2 Woe to those who make unjust laws, to those who issue oppressive decrees, to deprive the poor of their rights and withhold justice from the oppressed of my people, making widows their prey and robbing the fatherless.

Jeremiah 7:5–7 If you really change your ways and your actions and deal with each other justly, if you do not oppress the foreigner, the fatherless or the widow and do not shed innocent blood in this place, and if you do not follow other gods to your own harm, then I will let you live in this place, in the land I gave your ancestors for ever and ever.

Hosea 14:3 Assyria cannot save us; we will not mount warhorses. We will never again say "Our gods" to what our own hands have made, for in you the fatherless find compassion.

Zechariah 7:8–10 And the word of the Lord came again to Zechariah: This is what the Lord Almighty said: "Administer true justice; show mercy and compassion to one another. Do not oppress the widow or the fatherless, the foreigner or the poor. Do not plot evil against each other."

James 1:27 Religion that God our Father accepts as pure and faultless is this: to look after orphans and widows in their distress and to keep oneself from being polluted by the world.

Other Scriptures that mention the fatherless:

Deuteronomy 16:11   **Job 22:9**   **Job 31:17**   **Malachi 3:5**

Acknowledgements

*T*here came a point in my journey to get this book published where I truly believed it wouldn't come to fruition. After overcoming my *extreme* reluctance to ask for help, I dared to believe, and after a few weeks of stalling, I finally reached out to a few folks I believed would have my back, knew what I was working toward, supported me, and wouldn't mind sowing a financial seed so that I could finish the race and get this book published.

The response from you all brought me to tears. Literally! I am so full of appreciation (among other soft emotions) because if it weren't for you—who didn't hesitate to say yes—this book would not have been manifested. You all gave me the strength and resources to keep trudging along. And here I am.

Isaac Franklin	Johnnie Lewis	Ardell LeBlanc
Sasha Glenn	Eboni Lunsford-Evans	Matt Sherwin
Claudia Wood	Dorian Taylor	Amanda Jaskey
Stephenie Donnell	Marlyn Overton-Paolino	Rev. & Mrs. Kyles
Krystal Robinson	Rochelle Leeper	Leona Hunt
Krystal Brown	Alexis Howard	

From the very bottom of my heart, thank you!!

About the Author

*D*elmesha Richards is a native of Pittsburgh, PA, educated through the public school system and graduated from Perry High School in 1998. She left her "big city" of Pittsburgh to attend her beloved South Carolina State University, where she spent four years studying business management with an emphasis in IT, but she left school to relocate to Washington, DC, in 2002, where she began her professional career in IT at the National Institutes of Health in Bethesda, MD.

While immersing herself in her new career, it was important that she not spend too much time out of school, so she went back and earned her BS in business administration from Strayer University in 2005, and she has plans to never again step foot in another institution of higher learning—unless it's a totally paid for adventure toward a religious degree!

While climbing the corporate ladder in IT and project management, Delmesha eventually lost her zeal for the corporate workforce and ventured off into various entrepreneurial endeavors that allowed her to not only utilize her skills as a project manager and administrator but also opened the door for her teaching, creative and imaginative gifts to be released to flourish. Having a knack for grabbing life by the horns, she literally does whatever she wants. Her passions have multiplied and spread in a number of different areas, but one thing has always remained consistent: her love of communicating. Whether she's behind a microphone or behind a keyboard, you can find her discussing topics, ranging from faith and deliverance in Christ to racial inequality to the joys, frustrations, failures and triumphs of marriage and motherhood. She proudly declares that her superpower is *Truth*, which is why she is unapologetically transparent and incredibly honest.

Delmesha is joyfully married to her husband Ivan, and together they have three sons: Ivan Jr., Joseph, and Josiah. Her original plan was to have two boys and two girls, but apparently Jesus and Ivan missed that memo. Currently a stay-at-home-mom by day (and night, to be frank), she spends most of her time tending to her home and toddlers, managing her businesses, vlogging with her husband and now indulging in her writing and publishing career.

She's a textbook extrovert and loves connecting with people when she's not bogged down in family life (work life is recreational in her mind), so feel free to connect with her via

email: iamdelmesha@gmail.com

@iamdelmesha

@iamdelmesha

@iam.delmesha

Made in the USA
Middletown, DE
22 June 2019